THE ROUND DANCE OF KRISHNA
AND
UDDHAV'S MESSAGE

NANDDAS

THE ROUND DANCE OF KRISHNA

and

UDDHAV'S MESSAGE

translated with an introduction
by
R. S. McGregor

London

LUZAC & COMPANY LTD.
46 Great Russell Street
1973

SBN 7189 0163 0

Printed in England by Stephen Austin and Sons Limited, Hertford

PREFACE

Nanddās, who lived in the middle and later part of the sixteenth century, is one of the better known of many poets to have used the Hindi dialects of north India. His reputation is twofold. On the one hand, he is valued for the artistry of his verse, and for the learning with which he has treated different types of subject matter. On the other, his fame is as a devotee of Krishna. The preceding centuries had seen a long evolution of the worship of Krishna, who occupied a place second to none among India's gods; Nanddās's age was to see, perhaps, a culminating stage in that evolution, which it was his task and his fellow poets' to express to the people of north India. The following centuries, however, brought few innovations in devotional theology or in the form and style of devotional literature, and so it has come about that Sūrdās, Nanddās and the poetess Mīrābāī, in particular, have remained to the present day the chief north Indian exponents of Krishna devotionalism. The fact that they were active during the last truly creative period in the evolution of Krishna worship has given their poetry a special importance, and it should be of some interest to anyone wishing to appreciate the cultural background to modern India, or to understand the more traditional aspects of present-day Indian life. With this in mind, I have ventured to translate the principal works of a poet who has gone almost completely neglected outside the Hindi-speaking area of India, but whose compositions form a particularly good illustration of this cultural background.

By common consent the poems presented in this book are Nanddās's finest. The first describes Krishna's revels and dance with the herdgirls, whose passionate love is, essentially, symbolic of the soul's love for God. The second deals with the herdgirls' later separation from Krishna and their conviction of the value of their love for him, as compared with the futility of man's hope of salvation in following the arid 'path of knowledge', or the conventional ways of the world. These general themes are part of the common stock-in-trade of the Krishna poets, and between the sixteenth and twentieth centuries furnished scope for many different treatments in Hindi and other Indian poetry. The most popular style in north India was that of songs on isolated motifs, and in this Sūrdās, Nanddās's early contemporary, stands supreme. Nanddās's contribution was to produce connected treatments of the themes as a whole, treatments which are among the very first in literature in Hindi dialects, and which set out their subject-matter's significance much more clearly than a body of isolated songs could do: here was their original value, and here is the basic reason for their interest to us today. The first poem, *Rāspancādhyāyī*, is a version of the dance theme of the Sanskrit *Bhāgavata Purāṇa*, adapted to reflect tenets of Nanddās's sect, the dominant Krishna sect of north India. The second, *Bhramargīt*, presents the theme of Uddhav's message with considerable originality and crystallises the essential spirit of Krishna devotionalism as it was to be felt in north India from the sixteenth century onwards.

I have tried to write both for those who may pick up this book out of general interest, and for any who may have a more specific interest in aspects of Indian religion or literature. Of the translations I shall only say here that while they have been given verse form, they closely follow the sense of the original poems; a section of the Introduction provides some further information. The rest of the Introduction will, I hope, provide the reader with most of what he may wish to know about the poems, their author, and their background. It seemed right to give as much background information as has been done, since this could not be assumed to be readily accessible elsewhere, and in any case almost all the sources to which the reader could turn deal only incidentally with the Krishna literature of north India. Introduction and notes are both of course written with the Western reader in mind, but I hope the book as a whole may be of some interest in India also, especially to persons from outside the Hindi language area who would find a greater or less degree of difficulty in reading the poems in the original language.

To those persons who have assisted my work on Nanddās

I should like to express my appreciation of their help. My thanks go in particular to Dr. F. R. Allchin, who first drew my attention to Nanddās's *Bhramargīt* as a work deserving translation. I am indebted to him for his detailed comments on the *Bhramargīt* translation, from which it has greatly benefited, as well as for many discussions of questions taken up in the Introduction or having some bearing on it. I am grateful also to Mme Ch. Vaudeville, who kindly read the typescript in its final stage of preparation, and whose comments on a number of points made in the Introduction have likewise been to its great benefit. I need hardly add that responsibility for the opinions expressed in the Introduction and for the form and wording of the translations, as well as for any inaccuracies or errors which may occur in the book, is mine. My thanks go in addition to the National Museum of India for permission to reproduce the plate used as the frontispiece to the book, and to Srimati Madhuri Desai, the owner of the painting from which the plate was made. My last obligation is to my wife, for the interest and understanding with which she has followed, and aided, the progress of the work.

CONTENTS

PRONUNCIATION OF INDIAN WORDS AND NAMES

The following notes should give sufficient practical guidance. In the words and names as spelt, pronounce

a	as *u* in the verb 'subject'.
ā	*a* in 'father'.
i	*i* in 'sit'.
ī	*ee* in 'meet'.
u	*u* in 'put'.
ū	*oo* in 'food'.
e	French *é*.
ai	*a* + *i*, or as a vowel between the values of *a* and *e* in the words *man* and *men*.
o	*o* in French *mot*.
au	*a* + *u*, or as *a* in *all*, but shorter.
ṛ	*ri* usually. In a few words where *ṛ* is preceded or followed by a vowel it represents a 'flapped' sound, similar sometimes to English untrilled *r*.
ṭ ḍ ṇ	English *t*, *d*, *n*, or slightly farther back in the mouth as 'retroflex' consonants.
t d n	French *t*, *d*, *n*: 'dental' consonants, in which the tongue touches the teeth.
ṉ	*ṇ* or *n*.
k ṭ t p	unaspirated (as in *spin*, rather than *pin*, etc.)
c	*ch* in *church*, but unaspirated.
kh, *ch*, *ṭh*, *th*, *ph*	aspirated consonants.
gh, *jh*, *ḍh*, *dh*, *bh*	*g*, etc. + 'heavy' (voiced) *h* immediately following; as suggested by the names Egham, Edgeham, Odham, Cobham, written Eg-ham, Edge-ham, Od-ham, Cob-ham. In a few words of non-Indian origin, e.g. 'Mughal', *gh* may be pronounced as English *g*.
ś, *ṣ*	*sh* in 'ship'.
ṅ	*ng* as in 'sing'.

ñ	*ni* in 'onion'.
r	trilled slightly.
ḷ	'retroflex' *l*.
ḻ	'retroflex fricative *l*': the tongue tip is turned back and raised towards the palate (as would be suggested by a transliteration *zh*).
ṃ, *ṁ*	nasality of preceding vowel.
double consonants	lengthened.

Very many of the Indian words used in this book are Sanskrit words which are also current today as loanwords in Hindi, and other Indian languages. Final *a*'s and sometimes medial *a*'s in these loanwords are often not pronounced in Hindi; for instance, the name of the poet whose work is presented in this book would be, in terms of its Sanskritic origin, Nandadāsa, but is pronounced Nandădās with very faint *ă*, or Nanddās, by Hindi speakers. In Nanddās's own time final and medial *a*'s had not weakened to quite the extent found in the modern language. I have represented words which show this ambiguity of pronunciation in a modern form wherever it seemed reasonable to do so, i.e. in most cases where a word or name does not have a predominantly Sanskritic context. It was impossible to be completely consistent, however, nor did consistency on the point seem necessary since modern usage itself is variable.

The spellings are for the most part transliterations of the words as spelt in their original scripts, whether Sanskritic, Tamil or Perso-Arabic. Those of a number of words, including various personal and place names, have been modified in different ways for the general reader's convenience, the degree of modification often being greater in words of Perso-Arabic origin. In the translations the spelling *sh* represents both the letters *ś* and *ṣ*, and the same spelling occurs in the Introduction or Notes for *ṣ* (rarely *ś*), in words or names known to some extent in the West. *ri* and *n* are similarly sometimes used for *ṛ* and *ṇ* respectively. (These last three spelling devices, as it happens, are illustrated together in the English spelling of the word 'Krishna'.)

THE HISTORICAL AND RELIGIOUS BACKGROUND: A SURVEY

The historical background[1]

The early years of the poet known as Nanddās coincide fairly closely with the period of establishment of Mughal rule in India, and the years of his maturity with the rule of the greatest of the Mughal emperors, Akbar, in the latter half of the sixteenth century. Akbar's reign saw both the consolidation of the empire, and the inauguration of a period of relative stability and religious tolerance which was to be the norm, at least, for the best part of a century. The cultural climate of this period was to prove favourable to the production of many fine works of literature in Hindi dialects. Some of these works were composed by poets such as Bihārīlāl, Keśavdās or Abdurrahīm under the patronage of nobles or rajas at Hindu courts, or at the imperial court itself; others, including most of those of religious interest, were composed far from such centres of patronage, though not necessarily without private patronage or that of a Hindu sect. Nanddās's poetry is of this latter type, as is that of his famous contemporary Tulsīdās. It is clear that poetry in Hindi dialects, of whatever individual character, throve under the relatively liberal political and social attitudes encouraged during Akbar's reign and that of his immediate successors, and it can be no accident that the century 1550–1650 is the richest in the history of medieval Hindi literature.

The preceding centuries of Muslim rule had, from the point of view of the Hindu population of north India, for the most part been very different. The Hindus had learned to know the Muslims of Afghanistan first as plunderers, then as conquerors whose rule had usually been harsh. Their first

[1] The above survey is based chiefly on the following works: Percival Spear, *India*, Ann Arbor, 1961; V. Smith, *Akbar the Great Mogol*, Oxford, 1917; W. H. Moreland, *India at the Death of Akbar*, London, 1920; Ishwari Prasad, *History of Medieval India*, Allahabad, 1925; Abul Fazl, *Āīn-i-Akbarī*, translated by H. Blochmann and H. S. Jarrett, Calcutta, 1873–, 2nd ed. 1927–; Jahāngīr, *Tūzuk-i-Jahāngīrī*, translated by A. Rogers, ed. H. Beveridge, London, 1909; and others cited by Spear.

extensive experience of Islam came between the years 1000 and 1025, when Mahmūd of Ghazni repeatedly invaded and plundered north and west India, and the resentment and aversion inspired by these attacks is noted by the Arab historian al Birūnī, who was a contemporary of the events. In the late twelfth century Muhammad of Ghor, who had overthrown the Ghazni dynasty, seized its possessions in north-west India, and in the space of a few years he and his successors, profiting from dissensions among the Rajput chiefs, were able to capture Delhi and subjugate the whole of north India across to Bengal. The following century and a quarter saw much of Rajasthan, the Rajputs' stronghold, central, western and most of south India pass under the rule of the new sultanate of Delhi, and the imposition of a generally stern rule and harsh taxation on the Hindu population. It saw also, however, the beginning of the first important service Islam was to render India, her defence against repeated Mongol attempts at invasion, and if the Muslim yoke was heavy the presence of an effective military power in north-west India had clear advantages at this time. There is, too, especially during the reign of Firoz Tughlaq in the fourteenth century, evidence that the lot of the people was not an unrelievedly bleak one. Favour to Hindus was not unexampled. We read of a lightening of rents in Firoz's reign, of improvements in administration, and of building, irrigation and land reclamation projects which suggest improvement in conditions of life in his time. The use of Hindi dialects for poetry alongside Persian by the nobleman Amīr Khusrau (*c.* 1250–1320) shows, too, that some cultural approximation between Muslims and Hindus had taken place by this period, and foreshadows many valuable Hindi works by Muslims in later centuries.[2] Conversely, the

[2] Khusrau's non-Persian verses are in the rather mixed language which had come to be used in Delhi, based on dialects of the adjoining area, and called by the Muslims Hindi, or Hindui, 'Indian language'. This speech developed as a lingua franca current all over north India, or 'Hindustan', and later acquired the name Hindustani. From it evolved both Urdu and modern Hindi. Khusrau's language shows a certain influence, at least, from a cognate dialect, Braj Bhāṣā 'the speech of Braj', which belonged to the area south and eastwards of Delhi. Braj Bhāṣā, rather than the Muslims' 'Hindi', had inherited the main

rather casual or occasional interest in verses by devotional poets such as Nanddās or Tulsīdās, who were unattached to the court;[7] however, traditions exist of Nanddās and other poets of his sect being summoned to the emperor. Whatever facts underlie such traditions (which are discussed below) we can be sure that the norms which Akbar set for the organisation of Mughal society and his enlightened attitude towards the arts in general can only have favoured the work of such poets.

Of the physical conditions of Nanddās's India a certain amount is known or can be inferred from the statements of historians and travellers, and we can imagine something of the background against which Nanddās lived his life. The picture is one of great contrasts. Bābur's journal suggests that if India was a country rich in gold and silver, with splendid palaces and an aristocracy living a sumptuous life, the life of its villagers was one of stark simplicity. The European travellers who made their way into west and north India in the late sixteenth and early seventeenth centuries give the same general impression. Agra, and Akbar's shortlived capital Fatehpur Sikri, were then both larger than London, and thriving, prosperous cities. The same was true of Lahore and Ahmedabad. Trade by road and river seems to have been abundant, and this, with attachment to court or other patronage, the main sources of individual prosperity. On the

[7] It is true that tradition, e.g. as represented in J. Tod's *Annals and Antiquities of Rajasthan*, makes Akbar well disposed to the worship of Krishna, and even an admirer of the Sanskrit poetry of Jayadeva on the theme of Rādhā's love for Krishna; and again that Akbar is credited with the composition of Hindi verses, one at least of which mentions Krishna. On the other hand, if the famous Sūrdās was attached to Akbar's court, and yet receives no more than passing mention from Abul Fazl, poets unattached to the court are likely to have received little attention indeed, the more so when Abul Fazl does note the existence of the genre of *bishn pad* 'Vishnuite songs' of Mathura, the type in which Sūrdās excelled. Again, Abul Fazl's account of Hindu learning and scholarship makes no mention of the views of philosophers such as Vallabhācārya, the founder of Nanddās's Krishna sect, or of Viṭṭhalnāth, with whom sectarian tradition says he was familiar, despite the existence of Akbar's hall of worship which should have served as a forum for such views, had there been a great measure of interest in them. The historian al Badāonī, who might be expected to have mentioned any recognised division of Hindus to have influenced Akbar, likewise does not mention the sect.

teachings of Muslim Sufi mystics seem to have been favourably received by a large section of the Hindu population, with whose beliefs they in fact had much in common.[3] Such cross-influences brought about an increasing degree of interpenetration of Hindu and Muslim culture during the period preceding the arrival of the Mughals.[4] Clearly, the gulf between Hindu and Muslim was not unbridgeable. On the other hand, we read of Hindu uprisings in the fourteenth century and of the imposition of the *jizya*, a poll-tax on unbelievers, on brahmans for the first time, while the traveller Ibn Batūta tells us of Hindu support for rebel princes and governors in Muhammad Tughlaq's time (1325–51) and before, and of Hindu hostility and attacks made upon his party as it passed through the area around Delhi. It seems likely that although most Hindus must have lived law-abiding and peaceful lives under the Sultanate in these years, and at the level of everyday life toleration prevailed between Muslims and Hindus with many mutual cross-influences, members of the two communities must in the last resort usually have been as conscious of social, political and religious differences dividing them as of the interests they shared in common.

After Firoz Tughlaq the central power of the sultanate began to wane. In the aftermath of the invasion of the Turk Timur, in 1398, it disintegrated into a number of separate

literary traditions of older forms of speech. Partly for this reason, but also because the Krishna cult was centred on Braj, it was to become the vehicle *par excellence* of the Krishna literature of north India, including the poetry of Nanddās. Modern Hindi in turn finds its basic literary and linguistic traditions to a large extent in this literature in Braj Bhāṣā.

[3] S. M. Ikram, *Muslim Civilization in India*, New York, 1964, p. 124; Ch. Vaudeville, *Pastorales*, Paris, 1971, pp. 12 f., and 18, noting the sympathy of the Nizāmiya branch of Chisti Sufis with aspects of Hindu belief. This sympathy is well illustrated in the *Ruśdnāma* 'Treatise on Righteousness' of the Chisti, Abdul Quddūs (1456–1537), the Persian text of which includes over 100 Hindi verses illustrating beliefs of the Nāth yogi sect of Gorakhnāth; see the recent edition by S. A. A. Rizvī and Śaileś Zaidī, entitled *Alakhbānī*, Aligarh, 1971.

[4] Other factors favourable to this process were more general: the passage of time, bringing the birth of successive generations of Muslims in India, many of whom were of originally Hindu or part-Hindu parentage; also the fact that conversions of Hindus to Islam will often have been far from complete. This must have mitigated the strictness of attitude of many, not to say the majority of Indian Muslims. See Ikram, op. cit., pp. 130 f.

kingdoms and principalities. The fifteenth and early sixteenth centuries see attempts by successive dynasties to regain control of as much territory as possible, struggling constantly against kings and governors, and against a background of endemic Hindu unrest. A measure of centralised power was eventually established by Sikandar Lodī (d. 1517) and maintained by his successor Ibrāhīm.

The Lodī dynasty was overthrown by Bābur, a descendant of Timur and king of Kabul. Bābur entered India in 1524 and quickly established his claim to Delhi and his position as first Mughal emperor.[5] His son Humāyūn, in whose reign Nanddās was probably born, was not as effective a military leader as his father, and when Humāyūn's son Akbar eventually ascended the throne in 1556, a as boy of fourteen, there was still much to be done to consolidate the Mughals' position. As for the mass of the population in the central Mughal region, it would be surprising if they were prosperous, for the country had suffered repeated devastation in recent military campaigns. The short-lived Sūr dynasty of Afghan kings which had intervened during Humāyūn's reign had collapsed, after an efficient start, in confusion and administrative chaos, and in 1555–56 a serious famine had struck the Delhi-Agra area.

Akbar spent much effort early in his career in consolidating and expanding his dominions, and was vigilant in maintaining them. He was among other things a shrewd calculator of his interest. He saw that if the empire was to be soundly based it was essential that his Hindu vassals of varying grades (who could draw on substantial armed forces) should be won over to support it, and it was his conscious policy to involve them to some extent in its running. A sizeable proportion of his senior *mansabdārs* or administrators of crown lands were Hindus, as were certain of his ministers and many members of his court. His first wife was a Rajput princess. Quite early in his reign, and long before his rejection of

[5] The word Mughal or Mogul represents the name 'Mongol'. Bābur's claim to the throne lay in his descent from Timur, who, though a Turk, had come to be thought of rather in the same category as the Mongols whose efforts to invade India he had imitated (with rather more success).

Islam, he revoked the *jizya* tax and the taxes on Hinc worship. This was a state of affairs unexampled under tl sultanate. But Akbar's attitude here was more than one policy. It stemmed in part from a degree of interest in, ar sympathy for attitudes he found in his non-Muslim subjec This interest grew with time, and led him in 1575, perha ten years before Nanddās's death, to set up a special *ibāc khāna* 'hall of worship' in his new capital at Fatehpur Sil where religious questions could be discussed among membe of all faiths—Islam, Hinduism, Jainism, Zoroastrianism, ar Christianity, the last a recent arrival in north India. Sev years later Akbar established a spiritual order of his ow called *Dīn i Ilāhī* 'the faith of Akbar', based chiefly on Hin and Zoroastrian beliefs. He himself continued to rega Hindu rites and customs, and Hindu views in gener favourably, and until his death Hinduism remained officia at least in a favoured position in his empire by comparis with Islam. The *Dīn i Ilāhī* hardly survived his death, but t toleration and respect for Hinduism generated in Akba reign was to persist throughout those of his success Jahāngīr and Shāhjahān, and down into that of Aurangz

The range of Akbar's interest in the arts was, perha little less wide than that of his political and religious sy pathies. He was a generous patron of poets, artists, arc tects, musicians and singers both Muslim and Hindu (a himself studied singing under a Hindu teacher, Jahān tells us). Several important Sanskrit works were transla into Persian with his support. The excellence of Hin artists and the fame of singers such as Tānsen is noted by annalist, Abul Fazl. The latter also mentions a Sūrdās a singer attached to the imperial court, and it seems qu probable that this was the famous Hindi, or Braj Bhāṣā p of this name.[6] However, it is uncertain how far the cou actual interest in, or knowledge of the work of Hindu pc as such reached. Abul Fazl's long list of poets, as opposed singers, includes no Hindu names. It is likely that desp Akbar's evident partiality for various aspects of Hir culture, he and his court as a whole can have taken onl

[6] Vaudeville, op. cit., pp. 29 ff., and pp. 23 f. below.

teachings of Muslim Sufi mystics seem to have been favourably received by a large section of the Hindu population, with whose beliefs they in fact had much in common.[3] Such cross-influences brought about an increasing degree of interpenetration of Hindu and Muslim culture during the period preceding the arrival of the Mughals.[4] Clearly, the gulf between Hindu and Muslim was not unbridgeable. On the other hand, we read of Hindu uprisings in the fourteenth century and of the imposition of the *jizya*, a poll-tax on unbelievers, on brahmans for the first time, while the traveller Ibn Batūta tells us of Hindu support for rebel princes and governors in Muhammad Tughlaq's time (1325–51) and before, and of Hindu hostility and attacks made upon his party as it passed through the area around Delhi. It seems likely that although most Hindus must have lived law-abiding and peaceful lives under the Sultanate in these years, and at the level of everyday life toleration prevailed between Muslims and Hindus with many mutual cross-influences, members of the two communities must in the last resort usually have been as conscious of social, political and religious differences dividing them as of the interests they shared in common.

After Firoz Tughlaq the central power of the sultanate began to wane. In the aftermath of the invasion of the Turk Timur, in 1398, it disintegrated into a number of separate

literary traditions of older forms of speech. Partly for this reason, but also because the Krishna cult was centred on Braj, it was to become the vehicle *par excellence* of the Krishna literature of north India, including the poetry of Nanddās. Modern Hindi in turn finds its basic literary and linguistic traditions to a large extent in this literature in Braj Bhāṣā.

[3] S. M. Ikram, *Muslim Civilization in India*, New York, 1964, p. 124; Ch. Vaudeville, *Pastorales*, Paris, 1971, pp. 12 f., and 18, noting the sympathy of the Nizāmiya branch of Chisti Sufis with aspects of Hindu belief. This sympathy is well illustrated in the *Ruśdnāma* 'Treatise on Righteousness' of the Chisti, Abdul Quddūs (1456–1537), the Persian text of which includes over 100 Hindi verses illustrating beliefs of the Nāth yogi sect of Gorakhnāth; see the recent edition by S. A. A. Rizvī and Śaileś Zaidī, entitled *Alakhbānī*, Aligarh, 1971.

[4] Other factors favourable to this process were more general: the passage of time, bringing the birth of successive generations of Muslims in India, many of whom were of originally Hindu or part-Hindu parentage; also the fact that conversions of Hindus to Islam will often have been far from complete. This must have mitigated the strictness of attitude of many, not to say the majority of Indian Muslims. See Ikram, op. cit., pp. 130 f.

kingdoms and principalities. The fifteenth and early sixteenth centuries see attempts by successive dynasties to regain control of as much territory as possible, struggling constantly against kings and governors, and against a background of endemic Hindu unrest. A measure of centralised power was eventually established by Sikandar Lodī (d. 1517) and maintained by his successor Ibrāhīm.

The Lodī dynasty was overthrown by Bābur, a descendant of Timur and king of Kabul. Bābur entered India in 1524 and quickly established his claim to Delhi and his position as first Mughal emperor.[5] His son Humāyūn, in whose reign Nanddās was probably born, was not as effective a military leader as his father, and when Humāyūn's son Akbar eventually ascended the throne in 1556, a as boy of fourteen, there was still much to be done to consolidate the Mughals' position. As for the mass of the population in the central Mughal region, it would be surprising if they were prosperous, for the country had suffered repeated devastation in recent military campaigns. The short-lived Sūr dynasty of Afghan kings which had intervened during Humāyūn's reign had collapsed, after an efficient start, in confusion and administrative chaos, and in 1555–56 a serious famine had struck the Delhi-Agra area.

Akbar spent much effort early in his career in consolidating and expanding his dominions, and was vigilant in maintaining them. He was among other things a shrewd calculator of his interest. He saw that if the empire was to be soundly based it was essential that his Hindu vassals of varying grades (who could draw on substantial armed forces) should be won over to support it, and it was his conscious policy to involve them to some extent in its running. A sizeable proportion of his senior *mansabdārs* or administrators of crown lands were Hindus, as were certain of his ministers and many members of his court. His first wife was a Rajput princess. Quite early in his reign, and long before his rejection of

[5] The word Mughal or Mogul represents the name 'Mongol'. Bābur's claim to the throne lay in his descent from Timur, who, though a Turk, had come to be thought of rather in the same category as the Mongols whose efforts to invade India he had imitated (with rather more success).

Islam, he revoked the *jizya* tax and the taxes on Hindu worship. This was a state of affairs unexampled under the sultanate. But Akbar's attitude here was more than one of policy. It stemmed in part from a degree of interest in, and sympathy for attitudes he found in his non-Muslim subjects. This interest grew with time, and led him in 1575, perhaps ten years before Nanddās's death, to set up a special *ibādat khāna* 'hall of worship' in his new capital at Fatehpur Sikri where religious questions could be discussed among members of all faiths—Islam, Hinduism, Jainism, Zoroastrianism, and Christianity, the last a recent arrival in north India. Seven years later Akbar established a spiritual order of his own, called *Dīn i Ilāhī* 'the faith of Akbar', based chiefly on Hindu and Zoroastrian beliefs. He himself continued to regard Hindu rites and customs, and Hindu views in general, favourably, and until his death Hinduism remained officially at least in a favoured position in his empire by comparison with Islam. The *Dīn i Ilāhī* hardly survived his death, but the toleration and respect for Hinduism generated in Akbar's reign was to persist throughout those of his successors Jahāngīr and Shāhjahān, and down into that of Aurangzeb.

The range of Akbar's interest in the arts was, perhaps, little less wide than that of his political and religious sympathies. He was a generous patron of poets, artists, architects, musicians and singers both Muslim and Hindu (and himself studied singing under a Hindu teacher, Jahāngīr tells us). Several important Sanskrit works were translated into Persian with his support. The excellence of Hindu artists and the fame of singers such as Tānsen is noted by his annalist, Abul Fazl. The latter also mentions a Sūrdās as a singer attached to the imperial court, and it seems quite probable that this was the famous Hindi, or Braj Bhāṣā poet of this name.[6] However, it is uncertain how far the court's actual interest in, or knowledge of the work of Hindu poets as such reached. Abul Fazl's long list of poets, as opposed to singers, includes no Hindu names. It is likely that despite Akbar's evident partiality for various aspects of Hindu culture, he and his court as a whole can have taken only a

[6] Vaudeville, op. cit., pp. 29 ff., and pp. 23 f. below.

rather casual or occasional interest in verses by devotional poets such as Nanddās or Tulsīdās, who were unattached to the court;[7] however, traditions exist of Nanddās and other poets of his sect being summoned to the emperor. Whatever facts underlie such traditions (which are discussed below) we can be sure that the norms which Akbar set for the organisation of Mughal society and his enlightened attitude towards the arts in general can only have favoured the work of such poets.

Of the physical conditions of Nanddās's India a certain amount is known or can be inferred from the statements of historians and travellers, and we can imagine something of the background against which Nanddās lived his life. The picture is one of great contrasts. Bābur's journal suggests that if India was a country rich in gold and silver, with splendid palaces and an aristocracy living a sumptuous life, the life of its villagers was one of stark simplicity. The European travellers who made their way into west and north India in the late sixteenth and early seventeenth centuries give the same general impression. Agra, and Akbar's shortlived capital Fatehpur Sikri, were then both larger than London, and thriving, prosperous cities. The same was true of Lahore and Ahmedabad. Trade by road and river seems to have been abundant, and this, with attachment to court or other patronage, the main sources of individual prosperity. On the

[7] It is true that tradition, e.g. as represented in J. Tod's *Annals and Antiquities of Rajasthan*, makes Akbar well disposed to the worship of Krishna, and even an admirer of the Sanskrit poetry of Jayadeva on the theme of Rādhā's love for Krishna; and again that Akbar is credited with the composition of Hindi verses, one at least of which mentions Krishna. On the other hand, if the famous Sūrdās was attached to Akbar's court, and yet receives no more than passing mention from Abul Fazl, poets unattached to the court are likely to have received little attention indeed, the more so when Abul Fazl does note the existence of the genre of *bishn pad* 'Vishnuite songs' of Mathura, the type in which Sūrdās excelled. Again, Abul Fazl's account of Hindu learning and scholarship makes no mention of the views of philosophers such as Vallabhācārya, the founder of Nanddās's Krishna sect, or of Viṭṭhalnāth, with whom sectarian tradition says he was familiar, despite the existence of Akbar's hall of worship which should have served as a forum for such views, had there been a great measure of interest in them. The historian al Badāonī, who might be expected to have mentioned any recognised division of Hindus to have influenced Akbar, likewise does not mention the sect.

other hand the mass of the population, whether rural or urban, seems to have been poor, and ill-housed, and the peasants to have been often oppressively taxed despite Akbar's efforts to improve administration, while if food was for the most part abundant and cheap, there were no reserves when it grew scarce and prices rose. Famine was only to be expected. Following the famine of 1555–56, at least three others occurred in north or west India during Akbar's reign, and several outbreaks of plague or other epidemics are reported in the same period. It is clear that whatever the tolerance and enlightenment of Akbar's court, it brought little amelioration of the physical conditions of life for the mass of his subjects, both Hindu and Muslim. They could hope for, and must often have enjoyed, lives of freedom from want, but their hopes were not invariably rewarded.

It was against the political, cultural and physical background outlined in the above paragraphs that the various traditions of what is known as Hinduism moulded the attitudes and beliefs of the mass of the population. Hinduism was then, and is still today, more than a religion as such, for it seeks something more than to express and mould man's experience of the divine. To be a Hindu involved then, and to a greater or less extent still does today, living one's life in accordance with certain social conventions for which religious sanction is claimed. Among these was, for instance, the belief that birth determines the range of one's activities and duties in life, the range of one's potential marriage partners, and one's ritual status in society. Hinduism was thus not a religion in the sense of a fixed body of religious doctrine acknowledged by all its adherents, but a subtle, unhomogeneous amalgam of religious beliefs and social conventions which had evolved unsystematically over many centuries. For a Hindu, his Hindu traditions could well dominate his activity in most spheres of life, and it is for this reason that 'religious' texts bulk so large in the history of Indian literature. As for the Hindus of Akbar's time, we have seen that this was a propitious period for them in many ways, one which must have stimulated them to turn with revived confidence to their own traditions as an expression of religious and cultural identity.[8] It is in this general context that we have to see the devotional poetry of Nanddās, Sūrdās, Tulsīdās and other Hindi poets of the sixteenth and seventeenth centuries. Devotion, or *bhakti*, had in one or another form always been an important element in Indian religion, but only now did it reach its fullest expression in north India. Here it is directed chiefly towards the figures of Rām and Krishna, viewed often as avatārs or divine incarnations of a high god, Vishnu. The following pages trace the development of this Vishnuite, or Vaishnava, devotionalism, and of the particular Vaishnava sect to which Nanddās belonged.

[8] This is not to say that a continuing element of reaction against the frustrations of Muslim rule was not also present, one, perhaps, directed both against direct dominance, and against a certain tendency which Hindu society appears to have shown to turn in upon itself, with an increasing strictness of caste and family organisation, during the early Muslim centuries: a tendency working in the opposite direction to the interpenetration of Hindu and Muslim society which has been stressed above. The effects of this tendency upon the development of Krishna poetry are convincingly suggested by W. G. Archer, *The Loves of Krishna*, London, 1957, pp. 73 f. As far as the sixteenth century is concerned, however, the changed mood of north India is a new factor, and as is urged by Vaudeville, op. cit., p. 13, must have been of significance in the upsurge of devotional poetry in north India at this time. One may perhaps see a general parallel in the upsurge of confidence and achievement in Hindi and other Indian literatures following India's independence in 1947.

The religious background

1. *Vaishnavism: its development, and the worship of Krishna*[1]

Westerners are often impressed by what seems an abstract tendency in Indian thought, an emphasis on contemplation and philosophical detachment. There are good reasons, certainly, for this impression. The Vedic religion of the Indo-Aryans who invaded India in the late second millennium B.C. was transformed in India by philosophical speculation, which seems to have begun at an early date. Much of this speculation, which was of very varied character, was codified in due course in texts known as Upanishads, or 'sessions, (secret) doctrines', the earlier of which date from perhaps around 600 B.C. These Upanishads served in turn as points of departure for philosophical and religious speculation in later centuries. One doctrine stressed by the early Upanishads is that of the identity of the human self, or soul, with an ultimate reality—an abstract principle rather than a god, unqualified and impersonal, to which the name *brahman* was given. It was held that full and undoubting knowledge of the identity of the self with *brahman* obtained release for the soul from the cycle of birth and rebirth in the world, in which it was otherwise doomed to travel indefinitely in accordance with its *karma*, the merits acquired in each birth. Release brought a merging of the soul in the ultimate *brahman*. This belief became a central tenet of the orthodox brahmanical socio-religious system of the following centuries, and has remained of great importance down to the present day. From it, as much as from any single source, the element of stress on contemplation and philosophical detachment can be said to spring.

However, the Upanishads also contain passages which show that at a relatively early date the idea of affection for

[1] The above survey is restricted to those aspects of the religious background most relevant to the Krishna poetry of north India. It is based largely on the following works: R. G. Bhandarkar, *Vaiṣṇavism, Śaivism and Minor Religious Systems*, Strassburg, 1913; J. N. Farquhar, *An Outline of the Religious Literature of India*, London, 1920; J. Gonda, *Aspects of Early Viṣṇuism*, Utrecht, 1954; S. N. Dasgupta, *History of Indian Philosophy*, Vols. 3 and 4, Cambridge, 1949; J. E. Carpenter, *Theism in Medieval India*, London, 1921.

and devotion to a kindly, personal god, who loves men and offers them his grace, and is the object in turn of their loving devotion and reverence, was known in India. Feelings of this kind are referred to in one Upanishad by the term *bhakti*, and others suggest that it is the grace of god, as much as philosophical contemplation, which leads to union or 'participation' with the supreme soul.[2] These are theistic ideas, very different from the monism or pantheism underlying the philosophy of *brahman*. Such ideas are to be found in germ in the Vedic texts themselves, and, it must be assumed, were current among the Indo-Aryan as well as the non-Indo-Aryan population;[3] without doubt they are at least as ancient a part of Indian thought as the doctrine of the impersonal *brahman*, even though not stressed or presented as systematically in the Upanishads. They were held above all by the Bhāgavata sect, worshippers of a god named Vāsudeva and described as *Bhagavat* 'illustrious, adorable'.[4] From archaeological and literary evidence it appears that with this god there had by the second century B.C., at least, been identified both a beneficent Indo-Aryan deity called Vishnu,[5] and a figure named Krishna, in whom Indo-Aryan Vedic traditions must have mingled with a dominant component of originally non-Indo-Aryan belief at quite an early stage. Popular traditions of a cowherd god, such as Krishna becomes in later Hindu tradition, can be assumed to go back at least to the early centuries A.D., while the Krishna of the *Mahābhārata* epic is evidently of different origin, a semi-legendary, semi-divine hero, who comes to assume the role of avatār of Vishnu, and even that of the high god himself.

In the famous section of the *Mahābhārata* called *Bhagavad-*

[2] The word *bhakti* is connected with a Sanskrit root meaning basically 'participate in'. Relevant passages from Upanishads are: *Śvetāśvatara* 3.5, 4.11-, 6.21, 23; *Kaṭha* 2.20, 23 (=*Muṇḍaka* 3.2.3); translations in R. E. Hume, *The Thirteen Principal Upanishads*, Oxford, 1921.

[3] E.g. *Ṛg-veda*, VIII. 27.11, where the gods are praised for a *share* (*bhakti*) in good fortune; see J. Gonda, 'Het begrip bhakti', *Tijdschrift voor Philosophie*, Leuven, 1948, pp. 608 ff.

[4] The title is cognate with the word *bhakti*, and its basic sense is rather 'fortunate, prosperous'.

[5] Vishnu is a minor deity in the early Vedic texts, his nature that of a solar god or 'pervader'; Gonda, op. cit., pp. 172 ff.

gītā 'Song of Bhagavat', the mood of religious devotion or *bhakti* for this composite god, who is here called Krishna, finds its first clear expression. The *Gītā* plays a vital part in the development of theistic Hinduism, which, as far as texts are concerned, finds its beginnings here.[6] It strongly stresses the importance of *bhakti*, while endeavouring at the same time to make some accommodation or synthesis between its *Bhāgavata* theism and the Upanishads' monist teaching of the transcendent *brahman*, as well as with a separate, dualistic doctrine known as the Sāṅkhya system. Three *yogas*, 'disciplines or courses of action', leading to release, are regarded by the *Gītā* as complementary: those of *karma*, good action in terms of conscience and caste duty, of *jñāna*, abstract philosophical enquiry, and of *bhakti*. Of the three, that of *bhakti* is commended as the best, the simplest, and the most certain of success. The importance of the *Gītā* from our point of view is that in embracing this 'easier' way of *bhakti* it gave a broad base for the development of theistic views within brahmanical society as a whole, and also fostered a stability and organic strength in the outlook of that society, which must have assisted it during the following centuries in resisting, and ultimately so largely defeating the heterodoxy of the Buddhists and Jains. Again, in the realms of thought, its linking of *jñāna* and *bhakti* was to provide ample food for later speculation.[7] The importance which devotionalism was to assume within orthodox tradition—which was to become a Hindu tradition as theistic ideas received increasing emphasis—is well illustrated in the fact that the *Gītā* is at a later date very often itself described as an Upanishad.

The centuries following the *Gītā* see an increasing emphasis on the devotional attitude and various developments in theology. These confirm the emergence of a theistically-oriented Hinduism, superimposing itself upon the orthodox brahmanical system. Other gods than Vishnu-Krishna were here involved: in an appendix to the *Mahābhārata* called

[6] There are many translations and studies; e.g. by S. Radhakrishnan, London, 1948, and by R. C. Zaehner, Oxford, 1969 urging the relatively unitary nature of the *Gītā*.

[7] See verses 7.16–18.

Harivaṃśa, dating from perhaps the third or fourth century A.D., we find, for instance, explicitly stated the doctrine of the equivalence of the gods Śiva and Vishnu. There is a tradition of *bhakti* for a deity who was to emerge as Śiva implied already in the Upanishads, and a degree of mutual acceptance of Vishnu and Śiva by their adherents was evidently in their mutual interest. Again, Vishnu, Śiva and a third god, Brahmā, were now thought of collectively as aspects or manifestations of the supreme being—the *trimūrti*, or so-called 'trinity' of Hinduism. We find, too, that so-called *śākta* elements, involving the placation of goddesses invested with a divine *śakti* or energising power, soon come into prominence, chiefly in connection with the cult of Śiva. It is, however, with Vishnu-Krishna that we are directly concerned. Both in the *Harivaṃśa* and the *Vishnu Purāṇa*, a text which appears to follow it, we find important developments in the role of Krishna. From this point on, Krishna the divine but at the same time very human child and youth, who lives among the cowherds of the Braj district, near Mathura,[8] comes increasingly into his own. We now find the boy Krishna with his brother Balrām protecting the herds and herdsfolk of Braj from the attacks of demons and monsters, and in his youth enacting what was to be the most famous of his exploits: his sport with the ecstatic herdgirls and his round-dance, or *rāsa*, with them during moonlight autumn nights on the bank of the river Jumna. It is such themes, and the later motifs developed from them, which henceforward increasingly dominate the mythology of Krishna. Seen in this capacity Krishna frequently takes the name Gopāla 'the cowherd'.

With this change, a new emphasis begins to be evident in Vaishnava devotionalism: a rapturous, passionate strain of *bhakti* which is no doubt hinted at in the *Vishnu Purāṇa*, but

[8] Traditions of the cowherd Krishna very probably belonged to, and were transmitted by a nomadic pastoral people called *ābhīras* (cf. Hindi *ahīr* 'cowherd, cowherd caste'), who are mentioned in the *Harivaṃśa*. There are frequent references in Sūrdās's and Nanddās's poetry to the *ahīras* as worshippers of the cowherd Krishna. (The originally separate traditions of Vāsudeva were at the period described by the *Mahābhārata* known among the rulers of the Braj region, who belonged to the Yādava tribe or clan).

is very different in its scope, and different too from the *bhakti* enjoined by the *Bhagavadgītā*. It is to be seen clearly in the hymns of the Tamil devotees called Āḻvārs, composed perhaps between 650 and 850 in honour of Vishnu and his avatārs Rām and Krishna—but chiefly Krishna. The fact that these hymns are in Tamil, and that they propose *bhakti* as a path for all, outcastes and caste Hindus alike, suggests that the Āḻvārs' poems enjoyed a popular appeal matching the popular traditions of the cowherd god.[9] The name Āḻvār, based on a Tamil root meaning 'be immersed', expresses the intuitive, mystical tendency of their devotionalism.

The Āḻvārs' rapt devotion and mystical leanings are reflected in the epoch-making work which follows them, the *Bhāgavata Purāṇa*. This is again a southern work. It was compiled almost certainly in a Bhāgavata brahman community in the Tamil country and probably largely between 850 and 950. Written in Sanskrit, it may be seen as an attempt to make Krishna devotionalism and the Krishna legend more acceptable than they had evidently been to those who followed orthodox brahmanical practice and belief.[10] From our point of view its importance is, however, above all as a compendium from which are drawn the main traditions of Krishna devotionalism, as expressed in all the languages of India in later centuries, and as a matrix in which most of their lines of development are already present or hinted at. These functions, and the fervour with which it urges its message of devotion to Krishna, have made

[9] See J. S. M. Hooper, *Hymns of the Āḻvārs*, Calcutta, 1929. Confirmation of the earlier existence of these traditions in the Tamil country is found in the *Śilappadikāram* (trans. Ramachandra Dikshitar, 1939; A. Daniélou, London, 1967), a work which has been variously dated between the 2nd and 7th centuries A.D., but for which a fairly early date seems likely. The references here (chapter 17 and elsewhere) to Vishnu and to aspects of the Krishna story as later known suggest that the motif of a dance of cowherds and cowherdesses to a musical accompaniment, of popular origin, had earlier acquired a certain religious symbolism, and had begun, at least, to be associated with Vaishnava worship. The association is likely as yet to have been a tenuous one; cf. the evidence presented by Vaudeville in '*Kṛṣṇa-Gopāla* dans l'Inde ancienne', *Mélanges d'Indianisme*, Paris, 1968, pp. 737 ff. The importance of music and dance to the cult of the cowherd god is stressed by Vaudeville, *Pastorales*, p. 49.

[10] See essays by J. A. B. van Buitenen and Thomas J. Hopkins in M. Singer, ed., *Krishna: Myths, Rites and Attitudes*, Honolulu, 1966.

it one of the most influential books in India's whole religious history.

We are concerned chiefly with Book X of the *Purāṇa*. This presents the life and deeds of Krishna, against a vast discursive background in which cosmological and philosophical speculation, praise of the saints and other gods and an account of other avatārs of Vishnu all find a place. At roughly a third of the whole work in size it is clearly its culmination, and the frequent translations and adaptations of it which have continued right down to the present century show that it has always been so regarded. Now and henceforward we find an increased emphasis on Krishna the child and on his love for the herdgirls, but also, in the herdgirls' ecstasy and obsessive self-abandonment to Krishna, a noticeable difference in emphasis from the Sanskrit *Vishnu Purāṇa;* the *bhakti* urged so insistently by the *Bhāgavata Purāṇa* is on the whole more akin to that of the Ā..vārs' hymns.

It is not only Krishna the cowherd whom we find in the *Bhāgavata Purāṇa*, however. Even Book X gives considerable emphasis to Krishna the divine ruler and married husband, and the subject of Book XI is very clearly Krishna the supreme being. This is explained partly by the composite origins of Krishna himself, and partly by the origins of the *Purāṇa*, as noted above. We find the same thing in the *Purāṇa*'s teachings. As a whole, it places considerable emphasis on monistic ideas and negative definitions of the supreme being as 'the Self', 'the True Knowledge', *nirguṇa* 'unqualified', 'inactive', and so on.[11] But devotion is a sentiment, not a philosophical view, and the *Purāṇa's* stress on its importance carries some implication that the supreme being is positively qualified, or *saguṇa*, and is conceived of as personal. The fact that Krishna appears as an incarnation or avatār and is thought of at the same time as enjoying equal or superior status to Vishnu himself encourages this view. There is thus a certain paradox in the teaching of the *Purāṇa*, and a more prominent one than in that earlier syncretistic work, the *Bhagavadgītā*, where *bhakti* was not

[11] See A. Gail, *Bhakti im Bhāgavatapurāṇa*, Wiesbaden, 1969, especially pp. 22 ff.

defined so largely in terms of an ecstatic physical love. The paradox could, perhaps, be variously resolved, and the different attempts made to do so account for most of the attitudes reflected in later Krishna poetry, including those of Nanddās and his sect.[12] The success of the *Bhāgavata Purāṇa*, as of the *Gītā*, is that by the force of their conviction they manage to some degree to straddle such paradoxes, and to that extent fruitfully harmonise divergent elements of India's religio-philosophical inheritance.

The centuries following the *Bhāgavata Purāṇa* saw the appearance of several philosophers or theologians, all heavily influenced by the *bhakti* cult, if not necessarily by the *Purāṇa* itself. These philosophers were concerned to find support in the Upanishadic texts, or Vedānta, for the notion of a personal god which *bhakti* seemed to require. Since, as we have seen, support for this notion can indeed be found in the Upanishads, it is not surprising that they were successful in varying degrees, despite the contrary view of a predecessor, Śaṅkara, who had interpreted the same texts in a rigidly monistic sense; and we may rank the sects which they founded as important influences on the development of later devotionalism everywhere in India. The first to follow Śaṅkara was Rāmānuja, another southerner, who lived in

[12] It might be approached, first, at an intuitive or mystic level; here *bhakti* expressed in *saguṇa* terms would represent a striving of the spirit towards union with an ineffable being, transcendent but immanent in creation, whom it longs to love and to know perfectly, and at this level the devotee's ecstasies would contain the essence of both knowledge and devotion. One may speculate that the compiler or compilers of the *Bhāgavata Purāṇa* endeavoured to think of its overall 'message' in this way. At a different level, the straightforward idea of devotion for a *saguṇa* deity could be stressed (for the way of *bhakti* is certainly thought of as supreme by the *Purāṇa*). This would be possible especially where the devotee's attention was turned to the popular exploits of the cowherd god as an avatār. This approach would commend itself to the great majority of the devout. It would perhaps hardly appeal to those of a philosophical bent of mind, and would not necessarily appeal to those driven by intense spiritual longing, to whom consciousness of a *nirguṇa* aspect of the divine being would usually be of some importance. A more abstract approach, again, might content itself with distinguishing the complementary types of *saguṇa* and *nirguṇa* devotion (*Bhāgavata Purāṇa* III.29.7–12) without striving for an explicit synthesis; this is seen in Vallabha's theology. Nanddās in his poetry deals mainly with the *saguṇa* avatār Krishna, and commends the second of these approaches, though not without occasional references showing his approval of the others.

the 11th and early 12th centuries and systematised a philosophy of *viśiṣṭādvaita*, or 'qualified monism'.[13] According to this philosophy the *brahman* is not homogeneous, but contains elements of plurality; the soul can thus enjoy a qualified existence separate from *brahman*, which is not unqualified, unknowable, etc. as in Śaṅkara's view, but personal and possessed of all imaginable auspicious qualities, a true object for devotion. Rāmānuja's sect of Śrī Vaishnavas has been influential in South India. Some influence from his teaching may have reached the north through Rāmānand, a figure whose role and teaching are obscure. It is usually assumed that Rāmānand propagated a doctrine not of Vishnu and his avatārs, but specifically of Rām and his consort Sītā, and influenced in turn many important successors of different persuasion, including Kabīr, Nānak (the founder of the Sikh religion), poets in Gujarat, and the great Tulsīdās, whose work reflects a synthesis of theistic and other views of the same compelling kind as those of the *Gītā* and the *Bhāgavata Purāṇa* themselves. Apart from Rāmānuja, we must notice a second southerner, Nimbārka, who is believed to have settled in the heartland of Braj at Vrindāvan, probably in the early 12th century. Nimbārka put forward (even if he did not originate) an important contribution to Krishna theology in his theory of Krishna's celestial consort, Rādhā, thought of as reigning with him in a heaven of their own called Goloka.[14] Nimbārka's sect is

[13] Concise expositions of the views of Rāmānuja and the other philosophers mentioned in this paragraph can be found in Bhandarkar, op. cit., and in V. S. Ghate, *The Vedānta: a Study of the Brahmasūtras* . . . 2nd ed., Poona, 1960.

[14] The early development of the cult of Rādhā is unclear. A Rāhiya, i.e. Rādhā, is mentioned in conjunction with Krishna in the anthology *Gāhasattasaī* of Hāla, which may date from the 4th or 5th centuries A.D., and there are other early mentions predating Nimbārka; while a sect of Rādhā and Krishna seems to have existed in Bengal in the 11th century. See S. L. Katre, 'Kṛṣṇa, Gopas, Gopīs and Rādhā' (appendix), *P. K. Gode Commemoration Volume*, Poona Oriental Series 93, 1960, Part III, pp. 82–92; S. M. Pandey and Norman Zide, 'Sūrdās and his Krishna-bhakti', *Krishna: Myths, Rites and Attitudes*, p. 182; E. Dimock, 'Doctrine and practice among the Vaiṣṇavas of Bengal', ibid., p. 218.

Rādhā is not mentioned in the *Bhāgavata Purāṇa*, but mention of a favourite herdgirl probably reflects the existence of her cult in its time, see Vaudeville, *Journal of the American Oriental Society*, 1962, p. 38, conjecturing that the

said to have been especially influential in the Braj area itself, and in Bengal. Finally, at this approximate period, there is Madhva, again a southerner, and a devotee of Krishna, though not to the exclusion of other avatārs and gods. Madhva's system is a dualistic one, and his influence seems to have been greatest in western India; it is evident, for instance, in interpretations of the *Gītā* and *Bhāgavata Purāṇa* made by the Marathi-speaking Mahānubhāva sect, to whom we owe texts in this language from the late 13th century.[15]

The above paragraphs will have shown that on any view the development of Vaishnavism in the latter half of the first millennium and thereafter owes much to the south. Our evidence for north India for the period is fragmentary. The region seems by comparison to have been the preserve rather of traditions of brahmanical orthodoxy, of Śiva-oriented śāktism, a weakening Buddhist tradition (also *śākta*-influenced) and to some extent of Jainism throughout much of this period. It is clear, though, that Vaishnava *bhakti* was an influential force in north India in the 11th century. An allegorical drama called *Prabodhacandrodaya*, written shortly after 1050 in what is now eastern U.P., shows us the figure of *Vishnu-bhakti* defeating the forces of error, which include Buddhism and Jainism, and furthering the spread of views of a general monist kind; it is of interest that the supreme *brahman* is here equated with Vishnu, and that the avatār Krishna is specifically mentioned.

But along with the more staid type of *bhakti* evidenced here there coexisted a *bhakti* more akin to that of the *Bhāgavata Purāṇa*, centred on the herdgod Krishna. Al

Purāṇa's author or authors might well be reluctant to emphasise the cult, given their purpose. A connection is perhaps to be found with the Āḻvār poetess Āṇḍāḷ's Nappiṉṉai, implied in one poem translated by Hooper (op. cit., pp. 50–8) to be the bride of Krishna the cowherd (verse 29); and again with the *Śilappadikāram's* 'divine cowherdess' Piṉṉai.

[15] The famous Marathi commentary on the *Gītā* by Jñānadeva (1290) is not a Madhvan work, however, expressing rather monist attitudes suffused with and inspired by Bhāgavata *bhakti*.

For references to Mahānubhāva literature see I. M. P. Raeside, 'A bibliographical index of Mahānubhāva works in Marathi', *Bulletin of the School of Oriental and African Studies*, London, 1960, pp. 464 ff.

Birūnī had encountered the story of Vāsudeva, and some traditions at least of the cowherd god, and we have other evidence in occasional mentions of Rādhā from at least the 7th century; while Nimbārka's theology suggests its importance by the 12th century. Its first well-known expression in literature, however, is in the *Gītagovinda* or 'Song of Govind'[16] of Jayadeva, a poet attached to the court of King Lakshman Sena of Bengal towards the end of the 12th century. This famous and influential poem, composed in Sanskrit though probably modelled on the rhythms of vernacular poetry, first truly introduces the figure of Rādhā to the mainstream of Indian literature. Rādhā's is a varied symbolism in devotional poetry. She is, first, the chief and best of the herdgirls, which means that she is at once the most perfect of human lovers, and the most perfect in her devotion to the divine Krishna. On a different level, and especially in later poetry, she becomes the supreme *hlādinī śakti*, or joy-giving energy of Krishna, the means by which he feels the bliss which is the essence of his divine nature. The *Gītagovinda* is the story of her passionate love for Krishna, from whom she has become estranged, and with whom she longs for union. The earthy charm with which the tale is told does not quite conceal that it is intended also as an allegory of the soul's love and longing for the divine—a love that will not be mastered or put aside. The love of the other herdgirls for Krishna, as expressed in later poetry including that of Nanddās, is of essentially the same kind. Whatever the obstacles in their way, they will seek Krishna. At the sound of his flute on autumn evenings they leave household tasks, homes and husbands to join him in the groves on the bank of the Jumna. The mystic longing which impels them is something quite separate from questions of domestic, or social mores; if they were not so driven, after all, their love for the divine would be less than perfect. Thus it is that so much stress is laid in Indian literature on Rādhā and the herdgirls as *parakiyās*, women already married, who persist through the

[16] Govinda, a name of Vishnu-Krishna. The *Gītagovinda* is translated by George Keyt, *Sri Jayadeva's Gītagovinda: the Loves of Krishna & Rādhā*, 3rd impr., Bombay, 1965.

gravest of worldly obstacles in their quest for divine communion. If the quest is a frankly sensuous one, and its episodes sometimes suggest physical communion as much as divine, we must remember both that the stories of Krishna, Rādhā and the herdgirls are essentially popular ones adapted to a religious purpose, and the strength of the earlier *śākta* and *śākta*-influenced traditions against which they came to prominence in north-eastern India. Again, there is the probability already referred to that these stories answered a secular emotional need, assisting in the sublimation of psychological and social tensions which were on the increase during the early centuries of Muslim rule, and remained relatively strong thereafter.[17] But it would be a mistake to think of the Vaishnavas' Krishna poetry as essentially profane, even where it seems most dominated by a secular element. The repeated statements of later poets than Jayadeva make it clear that this was not the case; and the same can be seen here and there even of Jayadeva's Rādhā.

The centuries following Jayadeva saw a continuation in north-east India of the tradition of devotional worship and sensuous delight in Krishna, expressed above all through the figure of Rādhā. The Bengali songs of a poet named Caṇḍīdās, and those of Vidyāpati in the Maithili dialect of Bihar (14th–15th century) exemplify the trend. In these songs, the *śākta* and secular components of the Rādhā-Krishna theme are clearly evident. A further important development originating in Bengal occurred at the beginning of the 16th century, when an ecstatic visionary named Viśvambhar Miśra (1486–1533) founded a new sect based on passionate *bhakti* for Krishna, accompanied by adoration for a Rādhā now envisaged as herself divine, and his *hlādinī śakti*. This Caitanya sect, as it came to be called after the name assumed by its founder, extended its influence rapidly in Bengal and Orissa, and by 1516 had set up a colony in the sacred area of Braj at Vrindāvan.[18] Here in the following decades a theology was worked out for the sect, devotional

[17] See p. 8, n. 8.

[18] For its history see S. K. De, *Early History of the Vaisnava Faith and Movement in Bengal*, Calcutta, 2nd ed., 1961; *hlādinī śakti*, p. 281 and *passim*.

songs composed in Brajbuli[19] and Brajbhāṣā, and a restoration or re-creation of the sacred sites begun. A *bhakti* similar in its passion, though of a different cast in other ways, was coming to expression elsewhere in northern India at this period, for instance in the songs of Mīrābāī in Rajasthan, and Narsī Mehtā in Gujarat. It was this period, too, that saw another Krishna sect of north India, that of Vallabha, consolidating its position, and the production of its earlier literature, with which is associated the poetry of Sūrdās, Nanddās's famous predecessor. A discussion of Vallabha and his sect follows.

2. *Vallabha and his sect*

Vallabha was born probably in 1479. His family was from the Telugu-speaking region of south India, the same region from which came Nimbārka of Vrindāvan, by whom he was influenced. He appears to have travelled widely all over India propagating his views, to have come frequently to Braj, and established a temple to Krishna under the name of Śrīnātha, on Govardhan Hill, some miles west of Mathura.[20] For reasons which we shall have occasion to return to, his doctrines represent one of the last major revisions of the philosophy and theology of *bhakti.* They have probably enjoyed more influence in north India than those of any other Vaishnava theologian with the single exception of Rāmānand, and this influence is still active today.

Vallabha's teachings are based not only on the *Gītā* and Vedānta texts, but also on the *Bhāgavata Purāṇa*, which he

[19] Not in fact 'the speech of Braj' as the name implies, but a mixture of Vidyāpati's Maithili dialect and Bengali, with some Brajbhāṣā influence, used by Bengalis for Vaishnava lyrics.

[20] The available information about Vallabha's life is derived partly from Sanskrit texts, such as the *Vallabhadigvijaya*, as well as from traditions of the sect preserved in Braj Bhāṣā (see pp. 25 f.) These traditions are often conflicting, and since they are essentially hagiographical can only be used as possible historical sources with great reserve; see pp. 31 ff. A translation of some of the Braj Bhāṣā sources is provided by R. K. Barz in *Developments within the* bhakti *sect of Vallabhācārya according to sectarian traditions*, U. of Chicago, unpublished Ph.D. thesis, 1971.

Invaluable independent information on the history, topography and literature of Braj in general is given by F. S. Growse, *Mathurā, A District Memoir*, 2nd ed., Oudh, 1880.

regards as of equal authority. It has been conjectured that they rest to some extent on the doctrine of an earlier southern sectarian, Vishnusvāmī, but this connection is far from certain.[21] Many works are attributed to Vallabha, all in Sanskrit; the most important are a *Subodhinī* or 'elucidation' of the *Bhāgavata Purāṇa*, and a commentary on Bādarāyaṇa's *Brahma Sūtras* (both incomplete). From these and other works his doctrine appears as, essentially, a sort of inversion of Śaṅkara's monism.

For Vallabha the supreme being is not essentially unqualified or *nirguṇa*, as Śaṅkara would have it, and the phenomenal world, which Śaṅkara takes to be illusory, is ultimately real.[22] The supreme being, Krishna, is personal, and possessed of all imaginable auspicious qualities;[23] fundamentally his nature is three-fold, and is definable as *sat-cit-ānanda*, existence, intelligence and bliss. Among his powers is a supernatural *aiśvarya* 'almighty power', infinite, infinitely varied and ultimately unanalysable. Through this *aiśvarya* he obscures the *ānanda* and *cit* of his being in whatever ways he wishes, and so evolves from it all living creatures and the inanimate world. Living creatures partake basically of existence and intelligence without divine bliss, and the inanimate world of existence only, but all things are fundamentally of the nature of god, as sparks have the nature of fire. This monism, in which everything is positively defined, is given the name of *Śuddhādvaita* 'pure monism' to distinguish it from Śaṅkara's negatively defined monism. To it, such things as the old brahmanical cult, or the cosmologies of the Purāṇas, are in theory irrelevant, since all forms and processes may be referred finally to the supernatural

[21] Cf. Dasgupta, *History of Indian Philosophy*, 4.382–3, doubting the connection; H. von Glasenapp, 'Die Lehre Vallabhācāryas,' reprinted in *Von Buddha zu Gandhi*, Wiesbaden, 1962, pp. 193 ff.

[22] The above brief outline of Vallabha's essential doctrine is based chiefly on H. von Glasenapp, op. cit., and on the accounts of Bhandarkar and Ghate, with reference to Vallabha's *Ṣoḍaṣagranthāḥ* 'Sixteen Tracts', and to extracts from the *Subodhinī*, ed. M. G. Shastri, Samkheda, c. 1930.

[23] This Krishna, being personal and immanent, is *saguṇa*, though Vallabha retains the notion of a *nirguṇa* supreme being by stressing that his qualities are different from those of the material *guṇas;* they are not 'of this world', and Vallabha's supreme being is something other than the *saguṇa* avatār.

aiśvarya of Krishna. Vallabha does, however, make use of doctrines such as the theory of transmigration of souls and the Sāṅkhya *guṇa* system in elaborating the details of his own system.

The soul is regarded as imbued entirely by god as its *antaryāmī* or regulator,[24] and man is thus quite dependent on god for all thinking and perception. In accordance with this, the grace of god becomes of central importance, and a strong element of predestination is evident in Vallabha's teaching. God's grace is viewed as *puṣṭi*, a fostering, or tending the soul, a notion already present in the *Bhāgavata Purāṇa*. The full measure of his grace brings a consciousness of the divine bliss which is normally withheld from men, and salvation, visualised as union with Krishna in Goloka, the highest heaven. Vallabha's system is thus termed the *puṣṭimārga* or 'path of grace'. One may of course follow the path of *maryādā* or conventional life based on the Vedic scriptures, or the path of *jñāna* 'knowledge', though these can never themselves lead to the fullest salvation.

It is *bhakti* that leads to consciousness of bliss. *Bhakti* is open to all, and is unreservedly recommended. The ascetic life is of value only insofar as it may assist some to feel the yearning for Krishna felt by the herdgirls of Braj on the Jumna bank, or later, after his departure from Braj to the city of Mathura. In general, though, this sense of yearning is something accessible to all, and for this reason there is no emphasis on asceticism in Vallabha's system. Various categories of devotee and of grace are propounded, with varying relationships of grace to works; the perfect devotee, however, relies on grace alone. *Bhakti* is for him an inner compulsion, and any bliss he may feel in this world a fore-taste of future *sāyujya*, or immersal in God's being, which brings the delight (*rasa*) of union with him, or, even beyond that, the delight of savouring Krishna's own ineffable bliss. This is attainable, since devotee and deity are, after all, fundamentally one.

[24] The *antaryāmī* is thought of as a portion of the divine quality of bliss, which is otherwise withheld from the soul.

The *bhakta* should do everything possible to further the development of true *bhakti* within himself. He should seek the fellowship of likeminded persons, shunning unfavourable environments. By way of outward observation he should, for instance, praise Krishna in songs, listen to his legends, meditate upon him, deck and tend his image, worship, adore and serve him;[25] keep his festivals, wear his insignia, and go on pilgrimage to Vaishnava shrines throughout India. Above all he should place himself under the guidance of a good guru, if one is available.

Vallabha's teaching of Krishna's Goloka suggests the influence of Nimbārka upon him. It is noteworthy, however, that Rādhā has no place in his system, despite her being an important figure to the poet Sūrdās, who is claimed (though probably inaccurately) as a contemporary of Vallabha and a member of his sect.[26] She finds a place in the sect's official

[25] These outward observations, with the cultivation of feelings of intimacy with, and devotion to Krishna, comprise the 'ninefold *bhakti*' of the *Bhāgavata Purāṇa* (VII. 5. 23–4), which is referred to often by later Krishna poets and theologians (sometimes with adaptations). The cult of Rām accepts a different ninefold *bhakti*, see F. R. Allchin, 'The place of Tulsī Dās in north Indian devotional tradition', *Journal of the Royal Asiatic Society*, 1966, pp. 136 ff.

[26] Most historians of Hindi literature have seen Sūrdās in this light, following the sectarian traditions, and have discounted the possibility that a singer Sūrdās, mentioned in *Āīn-i-Akbarī* (completed 1597) as currently attached to Akbar's court, and the son of a celebrated singer Rāmdās of Gwalior, may be the famous Hindi poet. The latter tradition persists down to the late nineteenth century, however, where it is found, along with the tradition that Sūrdās was a pupil and contemporary of Vallabha (b. 1479?), in the anthology of Śivsiṃh Seṅgar, *Śivsiṃh saroj*, 1878 (ed. Trilokīnārāyaṇ Dīkṣit, Lucknow, 1966) on which much of the data of later literary histories have been based. Seṅgar, into the bargain, cites a date 1583 in connection with Sūrdās. His dates are in themselves very ambiguous, for the designation *u* which he uses seems to refer either to a poet's date of birth (*utpatti*) or to his having been alive in a particular year (*upasthiti*); in this case, however, he is surely suggesting that Sūrdās was alive in 1583. These facts and other considerations appear to support the recent argument of Vaudeville, *Pastorales*, pp. 29 ff., that the *Āīn's* statement is correct, and that Sūrdās was not a contemporary of Vallabha, or, probably, an initiated member of his sect: the absence of authentic references to Vallabha in his poetry (apparently confirmed by an allusion in the sectarian tradition itself, according to which Sūrdās is said never to have sung Vallabha's praise); parallel to this, the rather unspecific nature of his references to the importance of the guru, very different in tone and content from those of Nanddās, for example (e.g. ed. cit., nos. 416–17; 1792?); again, verses by him implying

teaching only from the time of Viṭṭhalnāth (1515–88?), Vallabha's son and successor, who was leader of the sect from 1548. Viṭṭhalnāth was without doubt influenced in his acceptance of Rādhā by popular belief of the kind reflected in Sūrdās, and perhaps also by the Caitanya theologians, who stressed Rādhā's importance, and who were active at Vrindāvan from well before the date of his accession; we find Rūpagosvāmī in his *Bhaktirasāmṛtasindhu*, for instance, equating the *puṣṭimārga* doctrines with his own, and the title of Viṭṭhalnāth's *Śṛṅgārarasamaṇḍana* 'Adornment of the Savour of Passion' suggests an emphasis in his teaching parallel to the tendency of the Caitanya Vaishnavas.[27] Viṭṭhalnāth's acceptance of Rādhā may, again, owe something to the rise of the Rādhā-Vallabha sect of Harivaṃśa (16th century).

We are told that Viṭṭhalnāth established his permanent headquarters at or near the village of Gokul in 1571, having first lived there several years previously,[28] and in Mathura

absence from Braj during a period of his adult life, at least (nos. 87, 1792; 1798?); and the fanciful sectarian tradition of his having reached an age of 125 years. It would appear that the famous Krishnaite poet, whose verse was of great potential value to the sect because of its popularity, was adopted by the sect and given a fitting place not only among its chief poets (see p. 25) but also on the doctrinal plane as a devotee and even a contemporary of Vallabha. This is not to say that Sūrdās was not influenced by Vallabha, or by parallel developments to his theology, perhaps arising within the popular *bhakti* tradition; and if his birth is considered as having taken place some few years after Vallabha's it is all the easier to account for the acceptability of his verse to the sect, and especially to Vallabha's successor Viṭṭhalnāth, with the latter's acceptance of the popular position of Rādhā. A statement in the sectarian tradition that Sūr conveys the spirit of Vallabha's *Subodhinī* commentary would seem merely to underline this point, rather than to prove a direct connection with Vallabha.

[27] See Rūpagosvāmī, *Bhaktirasāmṛtasindhuḥ*, transl. Bon Mahārāj, Vrindaban, 1965, p. 326. The Caitanyas emphasised the *śṛṅgārabhaktirasa* or 'savour of passionate love (for Krishna)' as much or more than the Vallabhans; cf. De, *Vaisnava Faith and Movement*, p. 203. An alternative term used by them, *ujjvalarasa*, is also used several times by the Vallabhan Nanddās. (For the word *rasa*, see further pp. 22, 44, 106.)

[28] Gupta, *Aṣṭchāp aur vallabh sampradāy*, vol. 1, p. 77. Gupta dates Viṭṭhalnāth's establishment in Gokul (from an earlier establishment in Aṛail, near Allahabad) at about 1566, instancing (but without details) an imperial grant of land apparently made to him at about that date. Viṭṭhalnāth may in fact

during an intervening period. It seems to have been Viṭṭhalnāth who first consolidated the organisation of the sect, stressing the position of the guru and the hereditary descent of the leadership, and instituting an elaborate cult of attendance on the god by the priest, involving the waking, dressing, feeding, etc., of the image in a 24-hour routine. A more important innovation from our point of view was his establishing a group of poets and singers called the *aṣṭ chāp*, the 'eight seals or insignia' of poetry—persons especially distinguished by his favour, or by the favour of Krishna himself. The sectarian tradition is that these poets all lived at Govardhan during Viṭṭhalnāth's pontificate, engaged in composing and singing hymns required by the cult, in producing other poetic works, or in taking part in the administration of the sect. Sūrdās and Nanddās are incomparably the finest. Their poetry will be discussed later; but we may notice here one effect of the use of Braj Bhāṣā for devotional verse by the *aṣṭ chāp*, and by other Krishnaite poets. It brought about a degree of familiarity with this dialect, and with certain conventions of literary and linguistic style, all over north India wherever Krishna is honoured, and this in turn furthered the use both of colloquial Hindustani, which is based on a cognate dialect, and eventually of modern Hindi, based on the same dialect, which looks back directly to such works as those of Sūrdās and Nanddās for its basic cultural and literary traditions.[29]

The later history of the sect need concern us little. Under Vallabha its influence had already extended into Rajasthan and Gujarat, and its position there was consolidated by his successors. Such information as we have about members of the sect comes largely from the hagiographies collected under Gokulnāth (*c.* 1550–1640) and his successors under

have moved to the region a few years before this date; Growse, *Mathurā*, p. 262 gives the date of his final settlement at Gokul as 1565, and dates relating to his journeys to Gujarat cited by Jagdīś Gupta, 'Brajbhāṣā ke gujarātī padpraṇetā', *Poddār abhinandan granth*, Mathura, 1953, p. 319, suggest a move to the region (Mathura?) before 1565. As will be seen, the period suggested by these dates forms the general *terminus a quo* for the bulk, at least, of Nanddās's poetry.

[29] See p. 2, note 2.

the name of *vārtās* 'chronicles'. Some of these *vārtās* no doubt do contain references which are in some form or another historical, and which bear on Gokulnāth's time, or on an earlier period, but their sifting from the hagiographic mass is a task yet to be undertaken.[30] During the reign of Aurangzeb the chief image of Śrīnāth was shifted from Govardhan to Nāthdvārā, near Udaipur in Rajasthan, where it still remains, and the sect is today based as much in west as in north India.

Before turning to Nanddās and his poetry, we may note the way in which Vallabha's views appear to have influenced the development of Krishna devotionalism in north India. Their distinctive quality is, as we have seen, their stress on the identity of the soul with the divine and on the essentially qualified (*saguṇa*) nature of the divine. With knowledge (*jñāna*) subsidiary, and stress now laid on the reality of the world and the dependence of the devotee on God, there must have been from the start a certain tendency for the Vallabhan devotee to overlook the reflective, contemplative elements of the Indian religious tradition which had been so fruitfully integrated with early devotionalism by the *Gītā*, and maintained in a fruitful, though different, combination with it by the *Bhāgavata Purāṇa*. The mystical approach to love allowed by the *Purāṇa* and encouraged by the ecstasies of Caitanya and his followers would perhaps not suggest itself so readily to the Vallabhan, and with stress laid rather on the *saguṇa* nature of Krishna as an avatār in this world the allegorical, or even the literal sense of the Krishna stories would tend to attract attention, since the world and everything in it could now be seen as ultimately real, even if falling far short of the perfection of Krishna's Goloka. In other words, there could often be a certain secularising tendency present, a relative

[30] The main *vārtās* are those gathered in two collections of 84 and 252, the *Caurāsī vaiṣṇavan kī vārtā* (ed. Dvārkādās Parīkh, Mathura, 1961) and *Do sau bāvan vaiṣṇavan kī vārtā* (ed. Brajbhūṣaṇ Śarmā and Dvārkādās Parīkh, Kāṁkraulī, 3 vols., 1951–3). There are many manuscripts and a number of printed versions. The two series describe figures said to have been closely connected with Vallabha and Viṭṭhalnāth respectively. Other collections of Vallabhan *vārtās* also exist.

restriction of the field of interest to an actual world, of which the divine world could be seen more as an extension than an idealisation. The Vallabhan emphasis on the position of the guru and the complicated ritual of tending the god's image may, insofar as they became exaggerated, be taken as reflecting this tendency. It would of course be quite unfair to impute any such tendency to Vallabha himself, who explicitly acknowledged a role for knowledge, even while subordinating it to love and grace, and to whom without doubt the concept of the *saguṇa* meant something very different from what it probably came to mean to some devotees. However, since Vallabha's doctrine of God's supernatural *aiśvarya* could now be used to account for the paradoxes of the earlier scriptures, there would in general have been little encouragement to further radical speculation within the sect.

It is probably largely for the above reasons that the pontificates of Vallabha, Viṭṭhalnāth and Gokulnāth during the 16th and early 17th centuries are the highwater mark of the Vallabhan movement, both organisationally and as far as its doctrine and literature are concerned. During this period the original impetus, and the collateral impetus of the Caitanya sect at Vrindāvan were still vital, and the splendid but baffling concept of god's supernatural might could still inspire. Gradually, however, it lost its compelling power, and with only relatively minor adjustments within the predominantly *saguṇa* Krishnaite doctrine now possible, the sect moved into a slow decline. It boasts no later theologians to equal Vallabha and Viṭṭhalnāth, and few later poets of great distinction; in literature the 18th century Gujarati poet Dayārām is indeed a justly respected figure. Organisationally too a certain decline appears to have set in, though the extent of such a decline has no doubt been exaggerated.

We must here again note the importance of the literature illustrated by the translations in this book. Throughout this period and down to the present day, the message of the 16th century Krishna poets to the people of north India remains an influential one, with its tale both of the joys to be found in life, and of the ultimate, divine reality beyond. Sūrdās stands pre-eminent in the people's estimation; Nanddās, more a scholar but no less a devotee, tells both of the fervent devotion of the herdgirls and of the teachings and interests of his sect. If, as is the case, later generations have valued such poets and their delightful message, their instincts have indeed been true to the ideals of Vallabhācārya.

NANDDĀS

Nanddās's life and works

Nanddās is known to popular tradition, or has been so known until recently, in the couplet

Aur sab gaṛiyā,
Nanddās jaṛiyā[1]
'The rest are as goldsmiths known—
As a jeweller, Nand alone'.

Little can be said with certainty about him as a person, however, or about the events of his life. In common with most poets of his time he gives almost no direct information about himself in his own poetry, and his contemporaries appear to make no mention of him, although a reference to a Nandanandanadāsa in a work which has been attributed to Sūrdās has sometimes been taken to refer to our poet and to suggest a date of birth around 1533.[2] The Muslim chroniclers, equally, are silent about him as about most Hindi poets, and this leaves Vaishnava tradition as the main source of information. We have seen that the Vallabhan side of this tradition is unreliable as it stands, though often it furnishes possible clues to historical fact. We are on much safer ground with Nabhādās's *Bhaktmāl* or 'Garland of devotees', a collection of verses giving information on many Vaishnava *bhaktas* up to the early 17th century. The *Bhaktmāl's* information is succinct and often hard to interpret. It deals, too, much more with matters of sectarian concern than with historical fact, but it is accepted as an authentic text and is our earliest external source of information about Nanddās. We learn from it of his skill as a poet

[1] Quoted by the anthologist Śivsiṃh Seṅgar, *Saroj*, p. 443, and others.

[2] E.g. by Dīndayāl Gupta, *Aṣṭchāp aur vallabh sampradāy*, pp. 260–1, 86–7. The reference is ambiguous, however, and the authenticity of the work concerned, *Sāhityalaharī*, far from certain; see Vrajeśvar Varmā, *Sūrdās*, Allahabad, 1959, pp. 104 ff.; Vaudeville, *Pastorales*, pp. 45, 47. Śivsiṃh Seṅgar, *Saroj*, p. 442, gives what appears to be a reference to a date of birth 1528 for Nanddās (see p. 23, n. 26, however, on the ambiguity of his references).

and wide fame as a singer; of the artistry of his works, dealing with both *bhakti* and the deeds of Krishna, and with rhetoric, or the art of composition; of his poetic temperament, and his connection with a village called Rāmpur. Other references are less clear. One, which has been taken by most writers on Nanddās to indicate that he was a brahman, seems to say merely that he was devoted to his fellow *bhaktas*. A second has been interpreted as stating that Nanddās had a brother called Candrahās, and this belief has worked its way deeply into the sectarian tradition as will be seen. But a more plausible interpretation of the reference is the rather different one that Nanddās was kindly and well-disposed to helpless devotees of Krishna.[3]

Later commentaries on the *Bhaktmāl* give no new information about Nanddās. An account of him by the Krishna poet Dhruvdās in his *Bhaktnāmāvalī* of about 1700 adds little in factual terms, though it fully confirms Nābhā's estimate of Nanddās's standing as a poet.

Nanddās's *padas* (verses for singing) contain a certain number of references to aspects of his life as a sectarian: his

[3] (*a*) Nābhādās, *Bhaktmāl*, ed. Bhagvānprasād Rūpkalā, 5th printing 1969, p. 696: *sakala sukula saṃbalita bhakta padarenu upāsī*. The word *sukula* cannot possibly indicate in this context that Nanddās was 'high-born' or that he was a Śukla brahman; the sense must be that Nanddās was devoted either to 'high-born' devotees, or more probably, those of 'good family' in the sense of belonging to a Vaishnava community.

(*b*) *candrahāsa agraja suhṛda*. Nothing is known of any 'Candrahās' who might have been Nanddās's brother, and there would therefore have been little point to a mention of such a person in the *Bhaktmāl*. The *Bhaktmāl* does, however, mention a legendary figure named Candrahās as a favoured devotee of Krishna, and it would seem that the reference here is a connected, though figurative one. In making Nanddās the *agraja*, or elder brother of Candrahās, the author of the *Bhaktmāl* is apparently saying that he is well-disposed to 'all Candrahāsas'. This interpretation squares well with that given to reference (*a*) above, and also with the fuller detail about Candrahās found in 12th century and later sources, where he appears, among other things, as an abandoned child of great promise, devoted to Krishna, who is taken under protection by adoptive parents. Krishna, it is said, is his real father and mother. In this context, a latter-day protector of the helpless devout might well be described as the 'elder brother of Candrahās'. The legend as given in these sources is set out by R. D. Gupta, 'The story of Candrahāsa as narrated by Priyā Dās and Jaimini and its comparison with the Kathākośa version', *Orientalia Lovaniensia Periodica*, Leuven, 1971, pp. 163 ff.

deep devotion as a Vallabhan to Viṭṭhalnāth and his son Giridhar, his daily singing of Viṭṭhalnāth's praise, his delight in dwelling with him in Vrindāvan, and desire always to be near the sacred sites of Braj. But the *padas* are silent on such things as his date of birth, family, caste or guru.[4] A few crumbs of historical fact or probability can perhaps be extracted from his words here and there, or even from his silences; several references to Viṭṭhalnāth suggest, for instance, that the latter was in permanent or semi-permanent residence at Gokul when the *padas* in question were composed, and these would then date from after the early or mid-1560's.[5] Again, he does not mention Gokulnāth, who dominated the sect from soon after the death of Viṭṭhalnāth in 1585, and it is likely then that he was not composing *padas*, at least, much after this date.

For further information we are restricted largely to the Vallabhan *vārtās* which contain the main traditions of the sect.[6] Many of these are no more than legend, or the work of imagination, but some very probably contain kernels of historical fact. They may do so even where this seems unlikely, for instance where the aggrandisement of the sect is sought by associating its members with the Mughal court in a way which, we have seen, must be at least exaggerated. Nanddās is said, for instance, to have been summoned to Akbar by the latter's minister Bīrbal after the emperor had heard one of his *padas* sung by the musician Tānsen, and,

[4] I have taken account here only of the *padas* which are stated to be preserved in manuscripts, not those preserved in later printed anthologies only. For further information see the two editions of Nanddās's works: Umāśaṅkar Śukla, *Nanddās*, 2 vols., Allahabad, 1942 and Vrajratna Dās, *Nanddās granthāvalī*, Banaras, 2nd ed., 1957; the former is more reliable on most matters. It records 35 *padas* preserved in manuscript, while the printed anthologies attribute several hundred to Nanddās. Some of the latter are very probably authentic; others are reworkings of apparently authentic *padas*, while some at least would appear to have arisen in support of later hagiographical traditions of Nanddās (e.g. Dās's no. 22, and perhaps 2–4).

[5] See p. 24, n. 28.

[6] The main *vārtā* traditions of Nanddās are in *Do sau bāvan vaiṣṇavan kī vārtā;* ed. cit., vol. 3, pp. 256 ff. A very helpful, though hardly sufficiently sceptical survey is given by Dīndayāl Gupta, op. cit., p. 140 ff.

even, to have died shortly afterwards in Akbar's presence.[7] It might seem pointless to attempt to use this tradition (as has been done) as evidence that Nanddās died by 1586, the year of Bīrbal's death, since the motif of his death in Akbar's presence is obviously a sectarian fiction. On the other hand, the years shortly preceding or following the establishment of the *Dīn i ilāhī* were likely ones for contact between Akbar and Vallabhans outside his court; Akbar was absent from his capital Fatehpur Sikri for more than a decade after 1585, and contact with the sect would not have taken place during these years, at least; Bīrbal and Tānsen were Vallabhans; and finally, most usefully where we are working with such wisps of evidence, there is the hint that Nanddās's composition of *padas* did not continue much after 1585. This congruence in dates may suggest that we should not dismiss the possibility of finding fact underlying some of the *vārtā* traditions, even where we are uncertain how they arose; and in the absence of contrary evidence we may perhaps provisionally accept Nanddās's death as having occurred by about 1585.

We may look in the same way at certain *vārtā* traditions which on the face of it do not appear to have aggrandisement of the sect as their aim; they, if themselves reasonable, would seem intrinsically more likely than others to be based on fact. A guarded acceptance may perhaps be given to the tradition that Nanddās came to Gokul only on his initiation to the sect by Viṭṭhalnāth, and that he had previously lived 'in the east', that is, somewhere east of the Braj area. His initiation would then have been in or after the early or mid-1560's, the period of Viṭṭhalnāth's establishment of the sect at Gokul. Less certain is the tradition that Nanddās had previously

[7] Op. cit., p. 279. Six of the eight poets of the *aṣṭ chāp* are said to have been brought before Akbar. Taken together the references in question are somewhat suspicious, in suggesting on the one hand relatively little knowledge of the sect on Akbar's part, and on the other relatively close contact with the emperor or court on more than one occasion (see especially the *vārtā* of Chītsvāmī, *Do sau bāvan vaiṣṇavan kī vārtā*, vol. 3, pp. 294 ff). If Sūrdās were at some point attached to Akbar's court, as seems probable, a basis could have been found in this fact for exaggerating whatever contacts between emperor or court, and sect actually took place; also in Bīrbal's and Tānsen's connection with the sect.

been a devotee of Rām as well as Krishna, since the few *padas* which might arguably support it are almost all of doubtful authenticity;[8] and the claim of brahman origin for Nanddās is far from certain, depending as it does principally on a misinterpretation of the statement in the *Bhaktmāl* mentioned above.[9]

We must now notice some traditions of a different kind found both in the *vārtās*, and elsewhere. These link Nanddās with the poet Tulsīdās, who composed his *Rāmcaritmānas* 'Holy lake of the deeds of Rām' in the mid-1570's, and they would seem to aim at raising Nanddās's prestige by associating him with his famous contemporary. Most are unverifiable, some manifestly spurious. We can reject, for instance, the notion that the two poets may have been brothers. So striking a fact would surely have been mentioned in the *Bhaktmāl*, whose author was a contemporary of Tulsī's. The tradition that Nanddās's *Dasamskandh* (an incomplete Braj Bhāṣā version of Book X of the *Bhāgavata Purāṇa*) was written in emulation of the *Rāmcaritmānas* is harder to assess. Without clear support it seems unlikely, as the two works, though superficially similar in scope, are really of very different kinds. On the other hand, a Vallabhan chronicler would hardly be likely to perpetuate a tradition showing the indebtedness of a Vallabhan poet to a non-Vallabhan in the absence of some basis of fact. Another *vārtā* tradition, according to which Tulsīdās visited Nanddās in Braj, receives limited support from a text giving details of Tulsī's life called *Gautamacandrikā*, apparently composed in 1624.[10] It seems clear that certain details given by this text are authentic, but on the other hand the published portion of

[8] One *pada* accepted by Śukla of clear Ramaite cast, ed. cit., vol. 2, p. 332, and Dās's *padas* 2–4, not noted in manuscripts. Such *padas* may suggest, if genuine, that Nanddās was a practising poet before his initiation, although the possibility of their being composed after initiation is not excluded. If not genuine, they most probably represent an attempt to connect Nanddās with the Rām cult for reasons suggested in the following paragraph.

[9] Another reason may be found in the fact that Tulsīdās was a brahman; see the following paragraph.

[10] Details of the *Gautamacandrikā* are given by F. R. Allchin, trans. *Kavitāvalī*, London, 1964, pp. 32 ff.

the text reflects a Krishna sectarian interest, and some details, such as those of a supposed journey through Vrindāvan, must be suspect on this count alone. If Tulsīdās did visit Braj, of course, a meeting between him and the *aṣṭ chāp* poets is very probable.

Finally, we may pass summarily over the other body of 'tradition' connecting Nanddās and Tulsīdās. This is a collection of manuscripts said to have come to light in Soron, near Etah in western U.P., in 1931, purporting to connect both poets with Soron and its neighbourhood and to give many details about them and their families, including the apparently fictitious 'Candrahās'. Those who have examined this material or parts of it have been almost unanimous in denying its authenticity because of inconsistencies in its evidence, and for palaeographical and other reasons.[11] There is every reason to agree. One imagines the same process taking place here as in the *vārtās*, one of attachment to Tulsīdās of traditions about Nanddās current in Soron, which has been conjectured, probably mistakenly, to be Tulsīdās's birth-place. (It may be added that a connection of Nanddās alone with Soron may be found in the fact that a village named Rāmpur lies only four miles distant; this is, again, 'east of Gokul', as required by the otherwise unsupported *vārtā* tradition of Nanddās's place of origin.)

A shadowy outline of the historical Nanddās emerges. A junior contemporary of Viṭṭhalnāth, he was born perhaps around 1530 and lived in a village called Rāmpur, east of Braj, possibly near Soron. He was initiated as a disciple by Viṭṭhalnāth, probably in the early or mid-1560's, and may have composed poetry before this date. Thereafter he lived very largely at least at Gokul with a reputation as a poet and singer and upholder of the *puṣṭimārg*. His active career as a poet is likely to have straddled the period of composition of Tulsīdās's *Rāmcaritmānas*. He died possibly within a few years of 1585, and by 1640 or earlier[12] various traditions about him had arisen and been consolidated within his sect.

[11] See for example Mātāprasād Gupta, *Tulsīdās*, Allahabad, 1946, pp. 93 ff.

[12] Nanddās is mentioned in a *vārtā* manuscript of this date, see Dīndayāl Gupta, op. cit., p. 130.

Over thirty works in all have been attributed conjecturally to Nanddās.[13] Perhaps no more than fifteen, however, apart from his isolated *padas*, are by the *aṣṭ chāp* poet. The determining of the authorship of small and little known texts, in particular, is complicated by discrepancies in researchers' statements about the existence, contents, readings and whereabouts of manuscripts and printed versions, as well as by the inaccessibility of most of the material; it seems likely, however, that some of the outstanding problems in connection with the canon of Nanddās's works will yield in time to investigation.

By far the most important of Nanddās's works are the two poems translated in this book, the *Rāspancādhyāyī* and the *Bhramargīt*. These, whose titles I have rendered 'The Round Dance of Krishna—a Quintet' and more freely, 'Uddhav's Message', are by common consent his finest, and it is chiefly for their fervour and brilliance that Nanddās is known and esteemed today outside sectarian circles. As is explained in the following pages, both are based on themes from the *Bhāgavata Purāṇa*, with different degrees of innovation. Apart from these poems Nanddās composed several others drawing from the *Bhāgavata Purāṇa*. His largest single work is the incomplete *Dasamskandh* already mentioned, which he apparently abandoned in its 30th chapter, very probably because he was dissatisfied with its progress and fairly humdrum style, and decided at this point to treat chapters 29–33, those dealing with Krishna's dance, in a freer and more lively way.[14] There are several short poems dealing with well-known individual motifs from the *Purāṇa*; those dealing with Krishna's rescue of his bride-to-be Rukmiṇī, and shorter, more pedestrian accounts of Sudāmā and Krishna, and the lifting of Mount Govardhan are usually

[13] E.g. by Gupta, Śukla, and Dās, opp. cit., and earlier writers there mentioned; Bhavānīdatt Upretī, *Nanddās*, Banaras, 1967; etc.

[14] Some *vārtā* traditions allege the loss of the bulk of this work; see ed. cit., p. 274; Dīndayāl Gupta, op. cit., p. 146 (mention of a different tradition, p. 141); also R. S. McGregor, 'Some manuscripts containing Nanddās's version of the *Prabodhacandrodaya* drama', *Journal of the American Oriental Society*, 1971, p. 492.

considered authentic. A further short work is the *Śyāmsagāī* 'The Betrothal of Śyām', composed in the same metre as the *Bhramargīt*. This diverges considerably from the *Purāṇa* in its treatment. Its heroine Rādhā does not figure in the *Purāṇa* at all by name, while Krishna's marriages in the *Purāṇa* are not to herdgirls but to princesses, Rukmiṇī and others, and represent a different side of the Krishna tradition. However, it is very probable that the cult of Rādhā was known to the author or authors of the *Purāṇa*,[15] and the poem can be seen as an attempt to present the popular figure of Rādhā as a *svakiyā*, a married wife, in distinction to the main tradition of Rādhā as a *parakiyā* and Nanddās's *padas* and other poetry which acknowledge her position as such.[16] Finally, among works based on the *Purāṇa*, there is the *Siddhāntpancādhyāyī* 'Quintet of Doctrine', sometimes known as *Rāsmanjarī*; this deals again with chapters 29–33, seeking to interpret the spiritual meaning of the *rās* dance in Vallabhan terms.

Nanddās also composed several works which reflect not only the general religious convictions of a Krishna *bhakta*, but also an abstract interest in theories of poetry and in the practice of the poet's craft. Clearly he was a man of learning, a scholar as well as a poet and devotee. His *Anekārthmanjarī* and *Nāmmanjarī* (or *Mānmanjarī*) are verse thesauruses giving synonyms or poetic senses of words in couplet or quatrain form, after the style of the Sanskrit *Amarakośa*, and intended for the use of poets and others not familiar with Sanskrit. Nanddās acknowledges this purpose and the *Amarakośa* as his ultimate model in the latter collection. In his *Rasmanjarī* he is similarly conscious of giving Sanskrit traditions a vernacular form. Here his theme is *nāyak-nāyikā-bhed*, the

[15] See p. 16, n. 14.

[16] The fact that the herdgirls of the *Purāṇa* long to marry Krishna (X.22.4) provides scriptural basis for this view of Rādhā. Again, Rādhā viewed as the *śakti* of Krishna is essentially a part of himself, and so may be considered as a *svakiyā;* the same is true of Nanddās's herdgirls, whose difference from mortal women and essential identity with Krishna he stresses. Like Nanddās, Sūrdās treats Rādhā not only as a *parakiyā*, but also as a *svakiyā* married to Krishna. The Caitanya theologians take a similar view of the herdgirls as *svakiyās*, and Rūpgosvāmī described Rādhā's marriage in his *Lalitamādhava*, completed by 1537; perhaps this, or a parallel popular tradition, served as a model to both Sūrdās and Nanddās. Cf. De, op. cit., pp. 348 ff.

detailed analysis of types of literary heroes and heroines, their emotions and the ways they are expressed, which had long been a subject of speculation and an ever-evolving theory among rhetoricians. This was potentially an important subject for the Krishnaite poets, preoccupied as they tended to be with the portrayal of the herdgirls' emotions. Nanddās works largely from the Sanskrit *Rasamanjarī* of the rhetorician Bhānudatta, and is one of the earliest poets in a long succession down to the 19th century to take up the subject in Braj Bhāṣā. As well as the *Rasmanjarī*, two other of his works show something of his interest in matters of rhetoric and technique, the *Rūpmanjarī* and *Virahmanjarī*; but these also strongly express a religious viewpoint, and can hardly be called rhetorical works as such.

Nanddās's works also seem to include a version of the Sanskrit drama, *Prabodhacandrodaya*. This work has long been lost sight of by historians of Hindi literature, but with manuscripts now having been brought to light seems genuine. Translated into Persian in the 17th century, it formed the basis of a new Braj Bhāṣā version by the Vallabhan Brajvāsīdās in the 18th century which remained important in Vallabhan tradition until modern times.[17]

Unfortunately none of Nanddās's works give any indication of date of composition. Some tentative inferences as to the likely order of composition of certain works are, however, possible. It seems very likely, as indicated above, that the *Rāspancādhyāyī* was composed after the *Dasamskandh*, and the relative stylistic maturity of the two works would tend to confirm this order. Stylistically, and as an inventive handling of its source or sources, the *Bhramargīt* would appear to belong to much the same period of Nanddās's development as the *Rāspancādhyāyī*; the *Śyāmsagāī*, in the same unusual metre, may not be far removed from it in time. The works showing a rhetorical interest on Nanddās's part perhaps precede those connected with the *Bhāgavata Purāṇa* as a group; the date 1567 which has been mentioned in connection with the *Anekārthmanjarī* does not seem to be

[17] See McGregor, art. cit., pp. 487 ff.

reliable,[18] but if, as seems likely, Nanddās entered the Vallabhan sect some time after earliest manhood[19] he would have done so as a person of some learning, and works reflecting this side of his nature might then have been expected to follow shortly after his initiation, rather than after an interval. The *Prabodhacandrodaya*, likewise a learned work, would also date well from this earlier period, probably not far removed in time from the *Rasmanjarī* and *Rūpmanjarī*, of whose language its introduction shows echoes, or from the *Dasamskandh*, a work of essentially similar scope.

[18] It seems to rest ultimately on Grierson's dating Nanddās as active around 1567; but this is merely his general estimate of the date of activity of the second four members of the *aṣṭ chāp*, taken as a group. *The Modern Vernacular Literature of Hindustan*, Calcutta, 1889, p. 20. Śyāmsundar Dās, *Report on Search for Hindi Manuscripts*, 1902, 1903, see *Anekārthmanjarī*.

[19] Cf. his probable date of initiation, *c.* 1560–6, with his traditional date of birth, *c.* 1530; the possibility that he was known as a poet before initiation; also a reference in the *Anekārthmanjarī* which has been conjectured to suggest that Nanddās had passed young manhood at its time of composition, Śukla, ed. cit., vol. 1, p. 102 (on *baya* 'age'): Upretī, op. cit., p. 48.

Rāspancādhyāyī: The Round Dance of Krishna

The subject of the *Rāspancādhyāyī* is, essentially, the soul's love and longing for God, matched by God's perfect love and grace. Nanddās unfolds this religious or 'spiritual' theme through the vivid human symbolism of the herdgirls' revels with Krishna on the Jumna bank, and in it expresses the delight which fills his whole being as a devotee of Krishna.

A summary of the subject matter of the poem will probably be helpful. Krishna, charmed by the beauty of the autumn nights of Vrindāvan, longs to dance his *rās* dance of communion with the herdgirls of Braj, and sounds his flute; the girls are enchanted by its supernatural music and abandon their mundane existence as wives and daughters of the herdsmen to make their way to him in the groves near the river bank. He is delighted by their beauty and welcomes them affectionately, but is conscious of their ties to the world, and of the fact that perfect love is not lightly attained, and urges them at first to return to their mortal homes and families. The girls reproach him for his harshness, reminding him that it is he who is the true reward of life, and that all creation is charmed by the sound of his flute. Krishna is now stirred by love, and runs through the groves to the river bank, followed by the girls. He sees, however, that their love for him is still tainted by selfish pride, and suddenly disappears from their midst, leading them in a state of despair. This completes the first section, or chapter, of the poem, which with its introduction is as large as the remaining four sections together. The second and third sections show the abandoned herdgirls scouring the woods for Krishna and imploring trees, creepers and forest deer for help in finding him. They come upon his footprints and those of a fellow herdgirl, whose supposed happiness they at first envy, and then rejoice in: soon, however, they discover her abandoned in her turn by Krishna. Returning with her to the river bank, they bewail their misfortune and Krishna's harshness, moved at the same time by compassion for his sufferings in his wanderings through the woods. Krishna now reappears among them, flute in hand; the girls welcome him ecstatically, and when they all sit down on the river bank, each of them thinks that Krishna is her partner alone. They question him as to the nature of love, and he is charmed by their devotion. The dance now begins, and the girls' ecstasy is matched finally by Krishna's own, and reflected in Nanddās's mood of rapt adoration as he evokes its details. At length Krishna and the girls rush into the Jumna to bathe. The poet takes leave of them at this point, adding concluding sentiments on the ineffable nature of the dance, the elusiveness of the divine realm of Vrindāvan, and the role of his poem in leading the devotee towards it.

This subject matter is, as indicated previously, far from originating with Nanddās. Almost entirely it is thoroughly traditional, looking back more than half a millennium to the *Bhāgavata Purāṇa*, and beyond that in part to the Āḷvārs and the ancient traditions of Krishna as Gopāl, the cowherd god. Both its outline and most of its details are to be found in the *Purāṇa* (Book X, chh. 29–33). A good illustration of Nanddās's dependence on the *Purāṇa* is to be found in the account of Śuka, its legendary narrator, with which he begins his poem; although this is not strictly speaking part of his subject matter at all, he nonetheless follows the *Purāṇa's* account (Book I, ch. 19) quite closely. It is true that he streamlines the *Purāṇa's* treatment, drops or alters the order or emphasis of various details and adds new imagery and interpretation of his own, but on the whole he adheres to the traditional account. We find the same thing with each of the main motifs of the story proper. His changes hardly minimise, if anything they emphasise his essential dependence upon the *Purāṇa* version of the story.

As if to emphasise further his dependence on tradition, we find that at some points where Nanddās's treatment differs from the *Purāṇa's* it is the same, or similar to that of Sūrdās. Sūrdās, whatever his date of birth, can hardly have been Nanddās's junior, and we know that Nanddās follows him in many details of his treatment of the *Bhramargīt* theme; a similar indebtedness is likely in the case of this poem. We may suspect that the praise of Vrindāvan with which Nanddās follows his account of Śuka, and which is an important structural element in his version, reflects to some extent Sūrdās's stress on the importance of Vrindāvan as the site of the *rās* dance, and that several long *padas* in which Sūrdās tells the entire story or its main episodes may have served as an incentive to Nanddās to compose a fuller, more faithful version. Again, a number of details of Nanddās's treatment are reminiscent of that of Sūrdās.[1]

There is little in Nanddās's version, then, that is not drawn from earlier prestigious versions, although we may readily admit his skill in adapting details of his received material. The real contribution of his poem to Krishna devotionalism lies in his interpretation of the traditional material, and in his poetic vision of it. The copiousness of the *Purāṇa* version allowed ample scope, after all, for selection and re-interpretation in accordance with individual taste, or with a sectarian view-point. Nanddās, as a Vallabhan, sets aside various aspects of it which conflict with his views and artistic purpose, stressing, synthesising and elaborating upon others.[2]

[1] E.g. aspects of the motif of the herdgirls' dejection on being asked by Krishna to return to their homes; and of their request to him not to urge the *dharma* of everyday morality upon them; at an artistic level, many details of the descriptions of the Jumna shore, the dance, and the power of Krishna's flute (some transferred from the context of Ch. 29 to Ch. 33). Sūrdās's treatments of the *rās* theme are in *Sūrsāgar*, ed. Nanddulāre Vājpeyī, 4th ed., Banaras, 1964, vol. 1, nos. 1606–1801; translated *padas* in Ch. Vaudeville, *Pastorales*, pp. 89–119.

There is some possibility of influence upon Nanddās from the Rādhā-Vallabha sect, e.g. on his description of Vrindāvan, see p. 108, n. to l. 100.

[2] For instance, he drops a long disquisition at the end of Ch. 33 of the *Purāṇa*, the main point of which was to stress the ultimately *nirguṇa* nature of Krishna; also most of the herdgirls' reasoning in Ch. 29 as to why they should not return to their homes, and certain passages of more abstract interest (Chh. 31, 32). He also reduces the *Purāṇa's* emphasis on the physical symbolism of the *līlā* at several points (e.g. at the end of Ch. 29, where the girls enjoy loveplay with Krishna before his disappearance, in Chh. 30 where they enact his deeds, and 33; see also note to l. 29 of the translation, p. 110). The point of many of his detailed changes (and the above omissions) is to concentrate attention on certain topics: the herdgirls and their love, which can come to full expression through the *rās* dance only; Krishna's love for the girls, symbolised by his gallantry and the power of his flute; the efficacy of worship of the *saguṇa* avatār rather than the impersonal *brahman* (indicated by his alteration of the motif of Parīkṣit's question, see p. 68 below; in the *Purāṇa* at this point Parīkṣit accepts that Krishna is the supreme *brahman*); again, the herdgirls' essential identity with Krishna (Chh. 29, 30); see p. 36, n. 16. Other changes are artistic, involving the reorganisation of motifs present in the *Purāṇa* version, or the introduction of new motifs of description (e.g. in the description of the Jumna shore in Ch. 29), or new details of metaphor.

A comparison of his version with the *Purāṇa* makes the differences quite clear, and we find confirmation of the theological views which influenced his treatment in his *Siddhāntpancādhyāyī*. On one important point, the position of Rādhā, they differ in emphasis from those of Sūrdās and are closer to Vallabha's. The prestige of Nanddās's poem rests on the poetic charm with which he expounds his view of the meaning of the *rās* dance, so central to Vallabhan teaching, and on the fact that it is the clearest and one of the earliest treatments of the theme in Hindi literature.

Nanddās is concerned above all to stress the importance of the herdgirls as the quintessence of love for the divine, and its most perfect human symbolism: their dance with Krishna is, then, the highest revelation which man can receive of his relationship with God. For their salvation all men must find the herdgirls' selfless devotion in their own hearts, for none but the herdgirls may go to Krishna. Their *prempanth* or 'path of love' is accessible to all, and supersedes the pandits' 'path of knowledge', and mortal men may hope to be transfigured by love just as they, and to find not *mukti*, release in the pandits' sense, but true self-realisation in love of Krishna. Nanddās emphasises that this love is, moreover, a delightful and a natural thing for man, and when once awakened, as is the girls' by the sound of Krishna's flute, leads the devotee unfailingly to him; the only condition is that it be constantly strengthened and purified, and not misused as a result of misunderstandings of its nature. It is not, of course, a purely physical love, although physical rapture is a meaningful component of it and deep human love is perhaps the only symbolism that can hope to give an inkling of its beauty. Nanddās stresses that the *rās* episode is not merely a *śṛṅgāra kathā*, an amatory tale, that Hari and his devotees are no mere sensualists, and several of his alterations to the *Bhāgavata* story are no doubt intended to help to avoid this charge.[3] The *Purāṇa's* message itself, however, is already clear on the point: the path of love, though bright, is a straight and narrow one, and even when Krishna is pursued most keenly he is all too liable to vanish far from sight. Perfect love

[3] Some details in above note.

leads to his embrace, however, as is symbolised in Nanddās's stress on the girls' transfiguration and abandonment of their own identity in that of Krishna.

Nanddās's Krishna reflects *par excellence* Vallabha's conception of the deity. In the *Siddhāntpancādhyāyī* he is the *saghana saccidānanda*, composed entirely of existence, thought and bliss, incomparable in his qualities, forms and powers, and the *parama dhāma* or 'supreme abode'. His flute voices the ineffable mystery of *brahman*, and the *rās* dance which he longs to dance with the herdgirls is the ultimate quintessence (*ekānta mahārasa*) of all scriptures and doctrines, its nature ultimately unknowable to man. His devotion to the herdgirls and delight in them is awakened by their love for him, even though he is himself *akhaṇḍānanda*, the perfection of bliss. It is these latter aspects of Krishna's nature and the promise of his love and grace which Nanddās stresses in the *Rāspancādhyāyī*.

It is interesting that both the *Rāspancādhyāyī* and the *Siddhāntpancādhyāyī* follow the *Purāṇa* in not mentioning the name of Rādhā, although both come rather close to doing so, when they use the verb *ārādhe* to describe the devotion of the girl Krishna took with him into the grove.[4] In Nanddās's other works the position is rather different. Rādhā figures by name several times in the *padas*, her *māna* or lover's pique is the motif around which the *Mānmanjarī* is built, and as already noted her marriage is the theme of the *Śyāmsagāī*. Sūrdās gives greater prominence to Rādhā than is seen in Nanddās's work as a whole, naming her time and again as Krishna's favourite with whom he dances in the middle of the ring of herdgirls, and hinting after the *śākta* fashion that his power depends on her as much as, or more than on himself.[5] Both Sūrdās and Nanddās, however, agree in not fully

[4] *Rāspancādhyāyī*, ed. Śukla, l. 335; below, translation, l. 526; *Siddhāntpancādhyāyī*, ed. Śukla, l. 169.

[5] See, for instance, *Sūrsāgar*, ed. cit., vol. 1, nos. 1678, 1783. Nanddās's verse reflects *śākta* influence less explicitly. The latter is fairly clear, however, in the concluding verses of the *Bhramargīt* (see below, p. 105); and in one of the *padas*, Śukla, ed. cit., l. 58, the concept of Rādhā as Krishna's *śakti* is transferred to the herdgirls, who are there represented as the *śakti* of Rādhā. See also notes to ll. 501 and 554 of the translation of *Rāspancādhyāyī*.

accepting Rādhā as a married *parakiyā*. In these facts we see on the one hand a popular standing enjoyed by Rādhā in north India which is not fully reflected in the *Rāspancādhyāyī*, and on the other a different approach to the significance of Rādhā's relationship with Krishna, intended to stress that all appearances to the contrary the couple are truly one. Nanddās shows us in the *Rāspancādhyāyī* a theologian's and a scholar's desire not to go far from the established doctrine of his authorities, the *Purāṇa* and Vallabha, and this despite the fact that he was an adherent of Viṭṭhalnāth, under whom the cult of a divine Rādhā is supposed to have first made official headway within the sect. We should not forget, however, that his unnamed herdgirls are to him very much what Rādhā is to her adherents, a symbol, if not a living myth, of supreme love and devotion. Hence there was no reason why his *Rāspancādhyāyī* should not continue to be an influential work as the Rādhā cult gained further ground in north India.

We have seen how far the poem reflects traditional influences in Nanddās's society: the general Vaishnava tradition of the *Bhāgavata Purāṇa*, and the more limited sectarian one stemming from Vallabha. Aesthetically too this is the case. The *Rāspancādhyāyī* lends itself well to appreciation in terms of time-honoured Indian criteria of literary criticism. In these terms it is worthy of praise for the way it evokes its pervasive mood, or *rasa*, of passionate love (*śṛṅgāra*), expounding the complementary situations of *viraha* (separation) and *saṃyoga* (union) in which the protagonists find themselves, and illuminating the theme by emphasising various *bhāvas* or emotions, and details of treatment which are judged conducive to awakening the *rasa* concerned; again, it is praiseworthy for the range and ingenuity of its *alaṅkāras* or 'adornments'—poetic conceits and assonances of language. Nanddās was thoroughly at home with this rhetorical tradition, and played a significant part with his work *Rasmanjarī* in mediating it to later writers in Braj Bhāṣā; his interest in the subject may have been stimulated by its importance to the school of Caitanya at Vrindāvan, in which, during his early years as it would seem, Rūpa had developed his influential theory of the *rasa* of *bhakti*, evocable through love for Rādhā or Krishna. This whole body of theory and its ramifications into devotional literature can no doubt be very largely taken for granted by the westerner making the acquaintance of a work such as the *Rāspancādhyāyī*.[6] It does, however, help to explain certain conventionalities of structure, and of imagery and expression, which will probably be noticed even in translation and which are encouraged in Indian literature by the long-established dominance of the theory. If the herdgirls' address to the forest trees seems unduly long and detailed, for instance, we must remember that Nanddās intends it to heighten perception of their plight in the situation of *viraha*, and that his auditors have so understood it. The description of the grove on the Jumna bank, again, seems to bulk large in its context, but must be seen, with the other natural descriptions, as an *uddīpana*, 'illuminator' or 'enhancement', of the prevailing *rasa* of love. At a different level one notes and must interpret correctly the conventional *sāttvika bhāvas* or descriptions of involuntary reactions, such as the sweating and ecstatic trembling so common in Indian descriptions of lovers, or again the apparent whimsicality of many poetic conceits, which are seen (if not violating the principles of *alaṅkāra*) as enhancing and extending the poetic atmosphere of the work and demonstrating the poet's versatility.

The *Rāspancādhyāyī* is perhaps memorable above all for its air of poetic charm. One thinks here of many themes and details, both from Nanddās's handling of the story as he received it, and also from among his innovations: of his description of the moonlight filtering through the leaves in the forest grove, for instance, or of the Jumna shore (where he goes far beyond the *Purāṇa's* details or Sūrdās's expansion of them); or among minor details, the description of the herdgirls' arrival in the grove; while old images, or their transference from one context to another in the course of

[6] The interested reader is referred to *An Anthology of Sanskrit Court Poetry*, transl. Daniel H. H. Ingalls, Cambridge, Mass., 1965, pp. 11 ff; S. K. De, *History of Sanskrit Poetics*, 2nd ed., Calcutta, 1960, and *Vaisnava Faith and Movement*, pp. 166 ff., 181 ff.

Nanddās's reworking of the story, lend their own novelty and would have played their part in holding the attention of a discriminating Vaishnava audience, even if they inevitably go unremarked by western readers. An aspect of the poem's charm is, again, Nanddās's skilful and suggestive use of language, which contributes vitally to the overall effect of his poetry. In his hands Braj Bhāṣā is a versatile instrument capable of expressing a very wide range of thought and feeling: from a devotee's heartfelt convictions, or the herd-girls' stubborn artlessness, to rhetorical subtleties or, drawing frequently on loanwords from Sanskrit, abstract concepts of religion or philosophy. Braj Bhāṣā, which already had a long if little-known tradition of literary use behind it,[7] reaches its peak in the literary language of Sūrdās, Nanddās, and their successors in the following century. Nanddās's technical skill in the use of this language is very clear in the varied assonances of his verse and rhythms of his metre, and well illustrates the brilliance in these fields also of which medieval Hindi poetry was capable.[8]

[7] See Śivprasād Siṃh, *Sūrpūrv brajbhāṣā aur uskā sāhitya*, Banaras, 1958; and p. 2, n. 2.

[8] Among studies of the *Rāspancādhyāyī* the interested reader is referred first to that in Dīndayāl Gupta, *Aṣṭchāp aur vallabh sampradāy*, vol. 2, pp. 823 ff. and *passim;* and to Bhavānīdatt Upretī, *Nanddās*, Banaras, 1967.

Bhramargīt: Uddhav's Message

Like the theme of Krishna's dance, that of Uddhav's message to the herdgirls appears in the *Bhāgavata Purāṇa*. Uddhav occupies a prominent place in the *Purāṇa* as a friend and devotee of Krishna; his devotion is, however, usually of a pronounced reflective cast, tinged with philosophical doubt and a tendency to see in Krishna the impersonal *brahman*. He is thus for the most part a *jñānī*, following the path of knowledge. His two chief appearances are in Book XI, where questions put by him serve as a pretext for philosophical disquisitions by Krishna, and in chh. 46–7 of Book X. Here he is portrayed as taking news of Krishna from Mathura to the people of Braj, who long for him in his absence; he consoles Nand and the herdgirls in his rather abstract fashion, and is charmed by the depth of the girls' devotion, which he longs to feel himself.

The figure of Uddhav is known to vernacular literature from at least as early as the beginning of the 14th century, the period of composition of a Marathi *Uddhavagītā* based on Book XI of the *Purāṇa*. Of treatments based on Book X, a Marathi commentary of about the same date is extant, and adaptations of the theme of Uddhav's message are found in Gujarati literature from the late 15th century onwards;[1] those of Sūrdās and Nanddās, however, appear to be still among the earlier in a long succession. Both Sūrdās and Nanddās give prominence to a motif not particularly stressed in the *Purāṇa*, in which the abandoned girls project their reproach and longing for Krishna upon a black bee which flies past, taking it in their overwrought state to be

[1] The Marathi commentary is mentioned by V. B. Kolte, *Bhāskarbhaṭṭ Borīkar*, Amaravati, 1935, p. 165. The Gujarati poet Bhīm gives a concise version of the theme of Uddhav's message in his *Śrī Hari ṣoḍaṣa kalā*, a digest of the *Bhāgavata Purāṇa* based on an intermediary Sanskrit version and dated 1484 (ed. A. B. Jānī, Baroda, 1928). A *Rasikagītā* dealing with the same theme may also be by this poet (selections in I. J. S. Taraporewala, *Selections from classical Gujarati literature*, Calcutta, 1924, 1, pp. 356 ff.). Bhīm is said by Taraporewala to have probably been a Vallabhan (i.e., at a later date than 1484); but cf. a later short study in R. C. Modī, *Bhālaṇ, Uddhav ane Bhīm*, Ahmedabad, 1944, pp. 60 ff. At least one other treatment in Gujarati, that by the poet Caturbhuj (1519?), precedes Nanddās and no doubt Sūrdās; see B. J. Sanḍesarā and S. B. Pārekh, *Prācīn phāgusaṅgrah*, Baroda, 1955, pp. 21 ff., 92 ff.

the messenger, Uddhav. This is the *bhramar-gīt* or 'bee-song', which is seen as a key to the significance of the larger theme of Uddhav's visit to Braj. Hence treatments of the larger theme, including the present poem by Nanddās, have themselves acquired the title *Bhramargīt.* Nanddās was certainly influenced in his treatment by that of Vallabha at a philosophical or theological level in his *Subodhinī*, and at a more popular level both he and Sūrdās probably owe something to the early Gujarati treatments, which show a broad similarity to their own. Their interest in the general theme may have been stimulated by the existence of Rūpa's Sanskrit *Uddhavasandeśa* (though this handles the theme rather differently), and at a sectarian level perhaps also by the tradition of commentary on the verses of the *Bhramargīt* proper which we know existed in the Caitanya sect shortly after Nanddās's time, at least.[2] The theme has enjoyed great popularity in Hindi literature from the 16th century onwards, having been taken up by Tulsīdās in his *Krishnagītāvalī* and *Kavitāvalī* and by several 18th century poets, and maintained its vitality even into the 20th century when, adapted and modernised to some extent, it has been used by such founding fathers of the modern Hindi literary tradition as 'Hariaudh', 'Ratnākar' and M. S. Gupta.[3]

Nanddās's *Bhramargīt* is more representative than any of his poems of the overall trend and balance of his poetry, and perhaps his own personality—devout, artistic, of somewhat

[2] The *Uddhavasandeśa* 'Uddhav's Message' is dated from before Rūpa's contact with Caitanya (i.e. before about 1514) by S. K. De, *Vaisnava Faith and Movement*, p. 646; D. C. Sen, *History of Brajabuli Literature*, Calcutta, 1935, p. 371. Verses from Narahari Cakravartī's Bengali *Bhaktiratnākara*, written in the early 17th century, indicate the standing of the *Bhramargīt* in the sect; text in Dineścandra Sen, *Vaṅga sāhitya paricay*, Calcutta, 1914, pt. 2, pp. 1254 f.

[3] On the place of the *bhramargīt* theme in Hindi literature in general, see Snehlatā Śrīvāstav, *Nanddās kā bhaṁvargīt, vivecan aur viśleṣaṇ*, Kanpur, 1962, and S. M. Pandey and Norman Zide, 'Sūrdās and his Krishna-*bhakti*', *Krishna: Myths, Rites and Attitudes*, ed. M. Singer, p. 192 f., 197; also Norvin Hein's recently published *The Miracle Plays of Mathurā*, New Haven, 1972, a study of a popular tradition of religious drama which was still current in 1950. The continuing cultural importance of the work of several devotional poets, including Nanddās, is clear from this study (see on pp. 179 ff. text and translation of a modern dramatic version of the *bhramargīt* theme employing a number of Nanddās's verses).

academic inclination. It gives, in addition, certainly the most attractive expression in Hindi literature of the views propagated by his influential sect.[4] To understand its emphasis we must look briefly at the *Purāṇa* account which is its source. As we shall see, Nanddās departs very considerably from this source, much more than in the case of his *Rāspancādhyāyī* version.

The *Purāṇa* starts with Krishna's request that Uddhav take news of himself to his fosterparents, Nand and Yaśodā, and the herdgirls, whose devotion has been so praiseworthy. Uddhav, duly welcomed by Nand and told of the grief of Braj, consoles Nand in terms which give considerable weight to the *nirguṇa*, unqualified aspects of Krishna recognised by the *Purāṇa:* Krishna is Acyuta, the imperishable one, without kindred, body or birth, who although unqualified, incarnates himself to protect the good, and to enjoy his relationship with man as expressed in the *rāslīlā.* Only on the following day does Uddhav appear among the herdgirls. The latter faint in delight, then on recovering weep and sing, at which juncture the *bhramar* motif is introduced. The girls reproach the bee for Krishna's faithlessness and cruelty, instancing his hard-heartedness as known from earlier avatārs, and long for his return. Uddhav feels himself greatly fortunate in meeting such devotees, and now delivers Krishna's message, which is broadly similar in emphasis to what he has already told Nand. The girls are not really separate from Krishna, and their apparent separation from him is intended only to intensify their love, and his for them; Krishna is the *sarvātmā*, the soul of all, and this soul is pure (*śuddha*), separate from and not partaking of quality

[4] This is not to say that the point of view of a Braj Bhāṣā poem such as the *Bhramargīt* corresponds exactly to that of the sect's theologians, Vallabha and Viṭṭhal, or to that of such a person as Nanddās himself. Certain references in the *Bhramargīt* suggest that even in composing this popular poem Nanddās may have looked beyond the doctrine of the *saguṇ* avatār which he advocates there (see notes to ll. 61, 167), and the tenor of the opening verse of the *Siddhāntpancādhyāyī*, where one would expect to find his own doctrinal position set out most clearly, suggests the same thing rather more strongly. The influence of Vallabha upon him has been mentioned. It is clear, however, that the sect as a whole moved in the direction of the point of view emphasised by the *Bhramargīt;* see pp. 26 ff.

(*vyatirikta, aguṇānvaya*). The girls receive this message with satisfaction, and pay their respects to Uddhav, voicing again their devotion to and dependence on Krishna and their feeling of hurt at being abandoned by him. Uddhav is now abundantly convinced of the worth of their *bhakti*, and after a stay of some months in Braj returns to give news of it to Krishna.

The *Purāṇa* is here recommending devotion to Krishna as a superior means of access to him, on the whole, than embracing the philosophy of the impersonal *brahman*. Nanddās's *Bhramargīt*, too, stresses the supreme importance of devotion, with Uddhav being won over by the herdgirls' *bhakti*, and eventually longing, as in the *Purāṇa*, to live in daily contact with them in Vrindāvan. But the *Purāṇa's* evident approval of the advice Uddhav gives the girls is not congenial to the Vallabhan Nanddās, and we find him reinterpreting its message, presenting Uddhav not as an uncritical spectator of the girls' devotion, but as the protagonist of views they disapprove of. In Nanddās's poem Uddhav is not a figure to be revered by the girls, but rather to be rebuked and corrected; only his final conversion is to be applauded. And the herdgirls themselves, while retaining most of the quality of *virahiṇīs*, abandoned women, are developed as opponents of Uddhav in a long argument beginning early in the poem as to whether the divine being is *saguṇa* or *nirguṇa*, qualified or unqualified, and what is the value of *karma*, action, and the mental and bodily discipline of 'yoga'.

If the girls will only look with the inner eye of knowledge, Nanddās's Uddhav tells them, they will see that Krishna is only apparently absent, for all phenomena share in the last resort the nature of *brahman*, which is impersonal and unqualified. The form of Krishna named Mohan, which so delights the girls, is thus illusory, and their beloved avatār Śyām is to be won by *yoga* rather than love, and by following the path of *karma* through an unending succession of rebirths. The girls deny these suppositions, insisting on the actuality of Krishna's deeds in childhood and youth and the ultimate physical or 'qualified' reality of the being who performed them. The doctrine of *karma* is at best a golden fetter—hampered by which one may certainly reach *svarga*, paradise, but never the heaven of Krishna which is found through love—and at worst it is an iron shackle from which there is no escape. To follow the round of *karma* can never be anything but a preliminary to the attainment of *prema*, love. And that absolute which is the goal of *yoga* has in the last resort a *nija rūpa*, an individuality of its own, just as does the hidden snake whose hole is worshipped by the householder. Śyām, then, is essentially a *saguṇa*, qualified entity, and although the illusion of *māyā* produces an apparently infinite variety of phenomena, these phenomena are all, in their different ways, fundamentally real, depending for their nature on the *aiśvarya*, will or power of God. Here above all, the herdgirls reflect Nanddās's Vallabhan convictions. Uddhav's remark that since no qualities of the ultimate being are known the Upanishads and Vedas may be right to term it *nirguṇa*, unqualified, is dismissed by the girls with the analogy that we lack knowledge of other qualities which do undoubtedly exist, such as those of the sun or moon; and they bring the discussion towards an end by asserting triumphantly that if Krishna is not subject to the laws of *karma* the latter must indeed be a fiction, and the very *nirguṇa* itself a *pramāṇa*, or mode of knowledge, of the *saguṇa*.

This interchange between Uddhav and the herdgirls can hardly be called a debate as such, because the passion of the girls' convictions and the doctrine of divine *aiśvarya* underlying them mean that no argument against the *bhakti* position is finally tenable, even if partial concessions to other points of view are made here and there. The dictates of reason and intellect alone, as symbolised by Uddhav's arguments, can only be acceptable insofar as they are not at variance with those of the heart and the emotions, purified by love for God. In his treatment of the *Purāṇa* theme Nanddās loses no chance to sharpen the contrast between Uddhav and the herdgirls so as to bring this message out more strongly, and most of his alterations to the *Purāṇa* version are made with this aim in mind. Thus he drops the entire first section describing Uddhav's visit to Nand, which in the *Purāṇa* appears at first sight to be Uddhav's main purpose, and begins without preamble with the confrontation between Uddhav and the herdgirls. Uddhav's consolation to Nand is addressed now to the herdgirls, supplemented with details from Krishna's message to them, which otherwise disappears. The bee motif which serves to stress the girls' longing and feeling of *upālambha*, reproach for Krishna, is relegated to quite a different position in the poem, Nanddās's intention being less to dwell on the girls' plight and their devotion than to use their confrontation with Uddhav as a device to allow a broad exposition of his religio-philosophical views. Again, he stresses the ecstasy of the herdgirls' love in a manner more reminiscent on the whole of the Caitanya sect, with its emphasis on the passion of the herdgirls and of Rādhā, than of the *Purāṇa*. And at the conclusion Uddhav is not made to stay on in Braj after his conversion, as in the *Purāṇa*, but returns at once to Krishna, fired with his message of the value of the herdgirls' *bhakti*.

Nanddās, then, sharpens and develops a doctrinal opposition barely present in the *Purāṇa*, certainly not explicit there, as well as stressing his conception of the importance of the herdgirls as catalysts of *bhakti*. As with the *Rāspancādhyāyī*, however, it was not he who originated the essential changes which appear in his version. In Vallabha's Sanskrit commentary on the *Bhramaragīta* verses of the *Purāṇa* we can already see the kernel of the argument between Uddhav and the girls developing, with the bee characterised as deceitful and a falsifier of Krishna's message. It was natural that Vallabha should read these interpretations into the *Purāṇa* text in view of his conception of the predominantly *saguṇa* nature of the divine being. However, the *Bhramaragīta* verses are to him still very largely of the nature of *upālambha*, interesting first and foremost for the light they throw on the abandoned herdgirls' emotions. Vallabha's views, or parallel interpretations which had arisen in popular tradition (such as those of the earliest Gujarati material mentioned above) were developed by Sūrdās, whose treatment of the whole theme of Uddhav's visit to Braj served in turn as a model for Nanddās.

Sūrdās's *padas* include two short connected treatments of the theme and a great number of isolated verses on individual motifs drawn from it, something approaching one eighth of the total volume of the *Sūrsāgar*. Like Nanddās, he stresses the importance of the herdgirls, both by making structural changes from the *Purāṇa* version and by putting the vast bulk of his *padas* into the herdgirls' mouths, and he frequently refers to the elements of the argument as developed by Nanddās: *nirguṇa* and *saguṇa* interpretations, the error of belief in *yoga*, the broken reeds of *jñāna* and *karma*. Uddhav is the victim of the girls' ire not because of his associations with the absent Krishna, as in the *Purāṇa*, but, anticipating Nanddās, because of the incorrectness of his views. The notion of an actual argument taking place between Uddhav and the herdgirls, too, is somewhat developed in Sūrdās's connected treatments of the theme. At the level of language and style, again, there are influences from Sūrdās's *padas* on Nanddās's phraseology, and one *pada* provides an exact model for the striking stanza pattern of Nanddās's *Bhramargīt*.[5]

On the other hand, the idea of the girls' separation from Krishna, and their *upālambha*, is still very prominent in Sūrdās, and comparatively little weight is given even in his connected treatments of the theme to abstract argument between Uddhav and the girls. The sections which present any type of argument are preceded, too, by long and generally more interesting ones on the girls' desertion and dejection. We may say, then, that Sūrdās expresses his conviction of the importance of devotion by emphasising the plight and constancy of the abandoned herdgirls, and in addition the firmness with which they hold to their *saguṇa* belief; it was left to Nanddās to build on this foundation.

[5] Sūrdās's *padas* on aspects of the *bhramargīt* theme are in *Sūrsāgar*, ed. cit., nos. 4030–4778; the connected treatments are nos. 4712–3 and 4714. Of many *padas* illustrating the girls' impatience with Uddhav's views, nos. 4141, 4193, 4196, 4223, 4227 are representative. The notion of argument between the girls and Uddhav is hinted at, in the isolated *padas*, in the sarcasm of such a verse as no. 4612, or 4604 with its preceding verses. A suggestive example of Sūrdās's influence on Nanddās is the wording of the first line of no. 4714, cf. the first line of Nanddās's *Bhramargīt;* again in 4374 on the deceitfulness of black creatures, cf. Nanddās's version, l. 231. No. 2236 shows the same stanza pattern as used by Nanddās.

Nanddās's contribution was to deal systematically with the abstract questions posed by the theme of Uddhav's visit to Braj, developing to its logical conclusion, for a Vallabhan, the contrast between *nirguṇa-* and *saguṇa*-oriented views of reality that was already clear in Sūrdās, and partially present even in the original source. His skilful and sensitive treatment throws much light on the nature of *bhakti* as a psycho-religious phenomenon, both on its more straightforward joy and delight in God, and on the all-embracing passion and visionary ecstasies towards which, especially in the Caitanya sect, it tends. His poem also helps us to grasp the cultural importance of *bhakti*, a credo at once simple and sufficient, which offers an essential spiritual independence, should the *bhakta* wish to accept it, from the dogmas and conventions of orthodox society.[6] Few if any poems in medieval Indian literature can be more worthy of our attention from this point of view. And the same poetic grace and charm which we have seen in Nanddās's *Rāspancādhyāyī* is again equally evident in his *Bhramargīt*, and must have contributed greatly to its influence in moulding religious and philosophical attitudes in the north India of his time, as well as to the popularity of the *bhramargīt* theme in later Hindi literature.

[6] Cf. verse translated on p. 102 below. A certain degree of practical independence of orthodox society might also have been hoped for, as the Vaishnava communities thought of themselves as to some extent separate from orthodox society. The openness of some, including that of Vallabha, to persons of low caste and to non-Hindus may have weakened the rigidity of the caste system as it affected individual members of the sect. However, any such tendency seems to have been more marked among followers of Rāmānand (see p. 16) than elsewhere, and it is uncertain whether, with the Vallabhan stress on organisation of sect and cult and the importance of the *guru*, later Vallabhans would have benefited to any great degree in this respect. The probable value of Vaishnava poetry as a sublimation of social tensions of different sorts has been noted above (p. 8, n. 8); a similar value of the *upālambha* motif as developed in Sūrdās and later poets is suggested by P. Gaeffke, 'Das Motiv der Gottesschelte in der neuindischen Bhaktiliteratur', *Zeitschrift der deutschen morgenländischen Gesellschaft*, 1969, pp. 924 ff.

Among studies of the *Bhramargīt*, the interested reader is referred first to the works mentioned on p. 46, n. 8, and to Snehlatā Śrīvāstav's above-mentioned study (note 3).

TEXTS, METRES AND THE TRANSLATIONS

Like most medieval Hindi poems, the *Rāspancādhyāyī* presents textual problems which mean that we cannot be quite certain of the number of verses it originally contained, or of some details of its wording. A considerable number of manuscripts exist, and are found to vary in wording to some extent, and in length very considerably. A number of printed versions have been made from one or another of these manuscripts, and there have been two editions in recent years by Umāśaṅkar Śukla and Vrajratna Dās, each based on a wide range of manuscripts.[1] The texts as printed in these editions are, however, far from agreeing. Dās accepts 211 verses, and gives readings which often seem to be corrupt and for one reason or another less likely to be original than others to be found in the manuscripts, while Śukla accepts as many as 301 couplets and gives what appear to be good readings. These discrepancies were proof that before a translation of the *Rāspancādhyāyī* was undertaken a study of its textual problems was essential.

From this study, of which details will be published elsewhere, it emerged fairly clearly that all the manuscripts used by the editors which give upwards of 300-odd verses represented a single broad recension 'A' of the MS tradition, going back in some form to an early date. A separate recension or possibly recensions (the evidence from the editions was not clear on this point) comprised all the manuscripts of 215 verses or less; the authority of these manuscripts was thus at least equal to that of the larger recension, and was enhanced by the age of some of them, and by the fact that most contained a significant number of better readings than those of recension 'A'. They were, moreover, quite numerous (10 out of 16 in all), despite the fact that the

[1] Details on p. 31, n. 4.

printed versions had popularised the longer text. Again, a great number of readings found in recension 'A' manuscripts were characteristic of recension 'A' only. The structure of the manuscript tradition and the readings of individual manuscripts thus combined to indicate strongly that the short version was original, but that early expansion of the text took place, followed probably by further expansion within the same recension, and Śukla's contention that the smallest size of version 'A' represents the original text seemed improbable on these fundamental textual grounds, which he had not taken into account. Śukla's argument that certain passages not in the short recension are essential to the continuity of Nanddās's poem appeared, moreover, highly doubtful in general, and incorrect in some specific instances, which were clearly interpolations; this meant that the possible number of original verses fell below the minimum number in the recension 'A' manuscripts.

Accordingly, I am confident that Dās's 211-verse text, which I have adopted following three of the manuscripts used by him and Śukla, closely reflects the number of verses in the original poem. The possible range of error is seen in the facts that the editors note four manuscripts from the short recension giving a few less than 211 verses (down to 206) and two giving more (212, 215); while a further one collated by me but unused by either editor gives 210. As to readings, I have adopted those of Śukla, since despite not recognising the short recension he consistently adopts readings from its manuscripts, and his edition seems a reliable guide to the wording of individual verses.

The *Bhramargīt* fortunately presents less acute textual problems than the *Rāspancādhyāyī*. There is no significant doubt as to the number of verses, 75 being attested by many manuscripts and printed in both Śukla's and Dās's editions. The verses dealing with the herdgirls' *upālambh*, and one or two others, are not all given in the same order in all manuscripts, and a fair number of variant readings are found; many accepted by Dās are evident corruptions. I have found Śukla's edition a more reliable and informative guide, and have followed it in respect of both readings and order of verses.

The metres used in medieval Hindi poetry can be classified under two broad headings according as they are structures of short and long syllables in a given sequence, or of metrical units or 'instants' totalling a given number. Nanddās's *Rāspancādhyāyī* and *Bhramargīt* use metres of the latter type. In these, a syllable containing a short vowel ranks as one 'instant' unless followed by more than one consonant, when it usually ranks as two (there are certain fairly standard variations involving the consonants *r*, *h*, and *n* and also the semivowel *y*); syllables containing long vowels or diphthongs rank as two instants. In the *rolā* metre of the *Rāspancādhyāyī* a line is composed of 24 instants, with a more or less strongly felt pause, which must coincide with a syllable division, usually after the 11th, or 13th; and lines rhyme in pairs, giving an *aa-bb-cc* . . . rhyming couplet pattern. The final two syllables should strictly speaking both be of the same number of instants, but this rule is frequently disregarded by Nanddās as by other poets. Other metrical licences also occur, particularly towards the end of lines where the count of instants seems to be less insisted upon, and in the position of the pause.

The opening lines of the *Rāspancādhyāyī* are as follows:

bandana karauṁ kṛpānidhāna śrī suka subhakārī
suddha jotimaya rūpa sadā sundara abikārī,

with pauses at the 13th and 11th instants respectively.

The closing lines are:

agha haranī mana haranī sundara prema bitaranī
nanda dāsa ke kaṇṭha basau nita maṅgala karanī,

with pauses at the 12th and 11th. Such lines as

manasija khelyau phāga ghumaṛi ghuri rahyau gulāla jyauṁ

or

aho mohana aho prānanātha sundara sukhadāyaka

show shortenings of the underlined syllables to count only one instant.

The metre of the *Bhramargīt* is an unusual combination of a *rolā* couplet with a *dohā* couplet, to which is added a coda. A *dohā* line is, like a *rolā* line, composed of 24 instants, but the distribution of syllables is more precisely regulated: there is a regular pause at the 13th instant, and there must be syllable divisions at the 6th, 10th, 19th and 23rd instants as well as at the pause. The three instants at the end of the first half-line must in addition not make a syllable pattern /–⏑/. The two lines of a couplet rhyme. The coda which follows the *dohā* is of 10 instants.

The second verse of the *Bhramargīt* illustrates the above:

kahyau syāma sandesa eka maiṁ tuma pai lāyau
kahana samai saṅketa kahūṁ ausara nahiṁ pāyau
socata hī mana maiṁ rahyau kaba pāūṁ ika ṭhāuṁ
kahi sandesa nandalāla kau bahuri madhupurī jāuṁ
sunau brajabāsinī.

The first verse follows a slightly different pattern in replacing the *rolā* couplet with a rhyming couplet of 21 instants in each line, and a pause at the 11th instant:

ūdhau kau upadesa sunau brajanāgarī
rūpa sīla lāvanya sabai guna āgarī
premadhujā rasarūpinī upajāvani sukhapunja
sundara syāma bilāsinī nava bṛndābana kunja
sunau brajanāgarī.

A probable model for this stanza pattern is provided by a long *pada* of Sūrdās's on the theme of the *dānlīlā*, Krishna's levying of a tribute of milk and butter from the herdgirls (ed. cit., no. 2236). Nanddās uses the pattern in one other poem, the *Śyāmsagāī*, with the single difference that the first verse of this poem has the same construction as all the others. Perhaps this different construction of the first verses of the *Bhramargīt* and the *Śyāmsagāī* can be traced to the fact that

Sūrdās's *dānlīlā* poem contains not two, but three couplets in its first verse, a 21 instant couplet, a *rolā* and a *dohā*.

I have tried to convey both the sense, and if possible something of the atmosphere of Nanddās's poetry. One might, perhaps, analyse this atmosphere in terms of an essentially simple poetic language, varied skilfully in texture by the use of Sanskrit loanwords, of a grace of sentiment and a conviction of devotion, and of a relative formality of poetic style. Such an atmosphere could probably not be suggested in prose, and it was evident that the problems of translation into verse had to be faced, even though a verse translation would almost inevitably be open to objections of one sort or another. It was clear, first, that the atmosphere of poems such as these risked being falsified if they were to be transposed exclusively into a modern poetic style, for from a modern Indian point of view they are thoroughly traditional in subject matter, style and language. They reflect not India's more modern composite culture as such, but an aspect of the traditional background to that culture. Their length and relative formality of style, in particular, suggested that it might be inappropriate to translate them into a modern style of verse, however suitable this might be for translations of short lyrical poems of the same period, with their very different atmosphere, or for translations of poetry of more secular type. On the other hand, there were difficulties in the way of more traditional verse forms also: English blank verse seemed over-formal and little suited to their themes and mood, and the use of rhyme and of particular metrical and stanzaic patterns had its own pitfalls. Nanddās's verse lines are rather longer syllabically and are liable to carry rather more sense content than any commonly used English line, as well as being capable of more metrical variation. After consideration, it seemed better not to attempt to use any standard line or stanza pattern systematically in translating them, despite the fact that both poems follow regular line or stanza patterns of their own. It seemed the more advisable, then, to seek what help could be had from rhyme and from the use of recognisable English metrical patterns in attempting to convey an impression of the poetry. I have aimed at a fairly homogeneous style of translation of the introduction to the *Rāspancādhyāyī* in the hope of suggesting at the outset, however imperfectly, something of the regularity of form of the original. In the *Bhramargīt* it seemed possible to use rhyme for a particular purpose in one series of verses, to suggest something of the atmosphere of the herdgirls' confutation of Uddhav. Rhyme was not, however, restricted to this section of the poem.

I have tried to bring out the sense of Nanddās's verses accurately and wherever possible explicitly. At some points I have been over-explicit, bearing in mind that the English translation should, ideally, be as easily intelligible to a person versed in English literature as the original to one versed in Hindi literature—or as much so as cultural and linguistic differences allow—and thinking the Western reader entitled to a hint as to the point of certain references in the translation itself, rather than merely in a note. But I have been fairly sparing with such hints. I hope that otherwise the translation contains very little which cannot be referred to details or to obvious implications of the wording, or to nuances of style present in the orginal verses. The converse problem of translation was that of avoiding the loss of shades of meaning clearly present in the original verses. It was always intractable, and was particularly acute where meanings and overtones could not be easily transposed because of cultural differences. Here more than elsewhere, losses and a measure of distortion seemed inevitable, even if one hoped that they could often be partially compensated for by an expansion in the text, or by a note. As one faced these and similar problems, conscious of their difficulty, many seemed in the last resort to be of a kind where hard and fast decisions as between alternative translations were barely possible. It was fairly clear, however, that while one tried to follow the literal sense of the original on a 'word for word' basis as far as possible, this did not always offer the best hope of expressing the essential meaning of a given turn of words as one saw it, or of a given verse as a whole.

THE ROUND DANCE OF KRISHNA: A QUINTET

I

The first of the five cantos opens with Nanddās's description of Shuka, the supposed narrator of the Bhāgavata Purāṇa.

I bow to Shuka, store of grace—
Beneficent and blest!
Whose form pure light pervades;
Who strays, by Hari's deeds obsessed,
Forever fair, and free
From fault, through the world delightedly:
No hill, nor other hazard stays
His passage—strange his ways!
His limbs glow fresh with youth—dark petals
Of some blue lotus—and his face their flower,
His trailing locks the bees that round it swarm:
His graceful brow—a host of moons—
Gleams broad and bright, its light
By his love for Krishna cast, that galaxy
Of suns, to banish night!
His eye, where compassion dwells,
Shines, somnolent and shot with red—
Heavy with the sweet draught of Krishna's sight;
His ear's a temple of delight
To Krishna; hair drawn back reveals
A graceful cheek, and honey's shed
In his slow smile, when love's bliss upon him steals!
A lofty nose, and a lip full and red,
With young moustaches elegantly spread
Between the two, demean
His namesake's shape and sheen;
At his throat, voluted lines
Unfold a parable of love for the divine—

Extinguish error, greed,
Anger, and lust, and pride!
His breast defies art's power to praise—
But the beauty it affords
Is most of all in Kānha's light, the lord's,
Undying in his heart;
And on the broad torso gleams
A sleek, rich line of hair, that seems
A rivulet, to draw delight
From his heart, as from a lake,
To the navel: there it streams
Into a hollow, deep and bright,
Whose folds three ripples on it make!
The arms reach to the knees; the knees
Are hid; the lordly gait awakes
A joy, which as he takes his way
Re-sanctifies each holy site
And Ganges doubly sacred makes!

The sun-jewel passed from mortal ken
When Krishna left the world of men:
Darkness rolled in upon his light,
Devouring folk and freehold; then
He saw their plight, and pitied them,
Revealed, so great his might,
The *Bhāgvat* bright!
Five chapters of this book contain
Its inner sense—a soul
To fill with life the whole,
As Shuka's song makes plain:
And now, at a friend's request, who lives
For Krishna's love alone,
I've told the self-same tale, as best
I can, in our own tongue!

Nanddās now describes Vrindāvan, Krishna's supernatural paradise.

Vrindāvan—who can tell
Its perfect beauty?
Limned of thought alone,
Its earthly counterpart a place
For Krishna to make known
His deeds to men—where beasts and birds,
Hills, groves and creepers, bushes, herbs
Are always lovely—free
From bonds of time and quality!
All creatures may repair
At will to him who's gentle as a deer—
Intent on Hari's deeds, devoid
Of anger, greed, lust, pride;
The sun shimmers, jewel-bright!
Each season's a spring renewed;
All earthly forests are suffused
With that paradise's light:
For Lakshmī, who ever tends
The Lord's feet in her form divine,
Gleams in each one, as is her whim—
Graces the world, it seems, now bright, now dim!
This splendour has no end!
No poet this greatness can define
(Though the Lord of his grace explained in part
To Sankarshan what it comprehends),
And as Ramā's joy, the blest
Nārāyan, is of gods the best,
Vrindāvan's supreme among forests—
Its beauty never wanes!
The sights seen in this forest
May grace no other ground—
As themes of verse confound
The very gods of poetry!
The soil is like the jewel that grants
To each his heart's desire;
All trees found in that forest

With Indra's wishing-tree compare:
The wishing-tree itself grows there,
Of glittering gems composed entire!
Roots, leaves, fruit, flowers one splendour share!
And the bees, drawn by their fragrance,
Charm with their murmur the very nymphs
And minstrels of the heavens' choir!
A mist of nectar breathes delight,
Hangs ever-brilliant in the air—
Fills with fresh life the fair Lover
When he turns from his dance aside;
And in that tree of paradise
A second marvel is seen:
Its branches, leaves, fruit, flowers bright
With images of Hari gleam—
Below, gem-laden, the soft golden ground
Enchants the heart,
Mirrors their light, and there, it seems,
A new Vrindāvan's found!

On a jewelled dais, that stands
A span in height, resplendent,
A lotus spreads its sixteen perfect petals,
Transcendental form;
The graceful seed-pod hangs
Above it, out of which all joy is born:
And there the young lord of Braj—
The mighty prince of lovers—is enthroned . . .

The beauty of Krishna is now described. This concludes Nanddās's introduction.

The auspicious jewel blazing on Hari's breast
Might shame a score of suns,
But pales beside its setting's loveliness—
Its light a mere star's seems:
For Mohan's strange form gleams
With baffling beauty,

Filling the firmament with Brahma's light!
He guides the beating of each heart—
The universal soul,
High spirit, primeval god,
Blessed one, righteous lord of all;
The beauty of the law divine
Is shown in Krishna's childhood form,
Then in the youth's, for ever young—
Kānha, who makes each heart his own!
This young Gopāl—strange herdgod—dwells
For ever in a place
Whose light outshines the splendour
Even of Vishnu's paradise!

The beauty of the autumn nights, and of the groves of Vrindāvan in which Krishna's revels take place.

The woods at every season
Enchant us, wild and lovely,
But in magic autumn win
Their rarest charm:
A priceless jewel's more brilliant
Worn in a splendid setting—
A handsome frame the nobler,
With ornaments adorned!
In welcome to the night
The jasmine, like a maid in youth's first flower
Unfolding, spreads her beauty,
Delicately bright,
And other flowers' lovely eyes
Shine, open wide,
As though fair Night, personified,
Smiles on the autumn groves!
The moon lifts up his train of stars—
Heralds the dance, and its delight,
A lover skilled, the face to gild
Of his beloved with saffron light;
His soft beams throw a burnished glow—

A haze, as of red powder hurled
By the god of love, to fill the grove
At this, his carnival!
The leaves, shot through with glinting rays
That slant to the forest floor,
Seem for Kāmdev a canopy
Made fast with crystal cord:
The moon slides high, an eager spy
Arrayed in beauty bright—
Peeks on tiptoe, to see the show
Now staged by Ramā's dear delight!

Krishna sounds his flute; the herdgirls go to him.

Then with his lotus hand
He raised to his sweet lips that flute
Whose melody all human power transcends;
Which cunningly transmutes
What never was, into reality:
Whose notes he subtly blends
To bring the sacred texts into our ken,
And in whose splendid form all happiness
Abounds—progenitrix
Of Brahma's unstruck sound!
The flute touched Mohan's lips, then sang
A song so sweet as to bewitch the hearts
Of the shy-eyed girls of Braj:

They heard it play! and now their way
To the melody they make,
Young wives, impatient of delay
At house wall, or tree-tangled brake;
Their path to immortality
Is bright—though very strait—
What other mortals may
That journey take?
Their bodies are the essence
Of love—ethereal, devoid

Of mundane quality, a light
To illuminate the world!
And those who stayed
Behind, afraid,
To earthly flesh were bound,
And won fair meed
Of every deed—
But the joy of love they never found!
  The others yearned for Lord Krishna,
Racked by longing, by hell-fire burned—
Each instant's torment seemed an age!
But when their mind's eye dwelt
Upon his dear form, held
In their embrace,
They knew the bliss of paradise untold,
Before which all joys fade!
What love should they have known
For Nanda's son, but love supreme?
Brass vessels, to that touchstone
Once laid, as gold must gleam!
So on their way of love they went,
Like young, bright birds till lately pent
In cages, flying free
From domesticity;
And none could stay their enchanted flight
Whose hearts were by Krishna ensnared—
A river's course might sooner
In *Sāvan*'s rain be barred!
The ornaments they'd thrown
About themselves, all disarrayed,
Had now to their proper places flown
As to their Hari they went their way!

Rajah Parīkshit questions Shuka as to the bodily reality of the herdgirls, and Shuka replies.

The king, Parīkshit, longs to learn
If joy knows any bounds

When in the *Bhāgvat*-jewel it's found,
And asks, for his peace of mind:
'Should one whom Kānha kept
Safe in the womb, O sage, then found
A pupil apt for the *Bhāgvat*,
A benefactor to mankind—
One in the tale of Shyām so rapt
That its beauty seemed ever new
(As tales of other's women hold
The ear of the libertine)—
Need one such put aside
This body qualified,
To find dear Hari, whom he's loved
As Kānha—not as Brahma known?'

And Shuka said
'My lord, the truth's well known
To those in whose hearts Lord Kānha dwells
—Who may all states assume:
The arch-villain, Shishupāl, might be
His lifelong, bitter enemy,
But won with ease felicity
Scarce known to holy men;
These herdgirls too, transformed by Hari's love,
Are not of womankind,
And dear to the moon of Govind's soul
As life itself, are their lotus eyes!'

The herdgirls meet with Krishna.

The jingling of anklets was so glad a sound to hear
That Hari's inner eye drew wide,
Strained out to reach his ear—
And when the gaily-tinkling train
Of herdgirls found their swain,
The senses drained from his body—
In sight alone they now inhered!
From face to face they fluttered—

And those eyes might well have been
Twin partridges, in restless wait
Under an autumn moon:
And the deferential faces
Of the herdgirls, as they thronged around,
Shone, like flashing lightning
Frames some dark, delightful cloud!
  And as the moon smiles soft and slow,
So smiled Nand's subtle son—
Spoke gallantly—and gallantry
Is love's criterion!—
For passion wears a gallant face,
And by a lover's art is graced:
Can gallant words be out of place,
Or thoughts, in fanning love?
  The girls were by his words beguiled,
Lost fawns, that through a thick wood file!
They softly smiled, and glances flashed
Sidelong, by bright eyes cast:
Fair schools of fish those eyes might be,
Flashing in beauty's sea!
But consternation spread
When Krishna said
That they should go
Back to their homes! And like a row
Of wooden dolls they stood,
And blankly gazed ahead!
Then their shapely necks like yielding lotus-stems inclined—
So great a load of grief oppressed their minds,
And their clustered lotus faces were by the weight drawn down
Of hair that hung, as bees might swarm around:
The sighs they drew were by the fire of separation fed,
And withered the sweet blossoms of their lips so full and red!
  And Giridhar was glad
When now, thrilling with love for their dear Mohan,
These girls of Braj spoke gracefully

And said:
'Why, lovely Mohan!—Lord
Of our lives! Giver of joy!—
Don't speak so harshly—words
Like these your names belie!
Speak of men's duty when you find
That they're to hear your words inclined,
But only then—why plague them, dear,
With talk they've not asked to hear?
A life lived as the Law decrees
Brings fit reward, all men agree;
So with their vows, austerities,
And calling on God's name—
The end result's the same!
But *you* are this life's true reward:
Who thinks to hear you speak of Law?
For at your beauty's charms
The Law itself forgets its norms,
And women's household duties seem
To them mere senseless forms;
The hills rise in delight, and flee
Their age-old immobility!
And creatures all that swim or crawl,
With beasts both wild and tame,
And birds, from food abstain:
If so, can girls be found
Who, hearing Krishna's flute's sweet sound
By those lips blown,
Would never shun
The Law?—In these three worlds, not one!'

The Lover heard their words, and felt
Within his soul love's smart,
And as in fire's heat butter melts,
So melts his tender heart;
And Nandlāl turned and smiled, and saw
The girls of Braj distraught,
And now, though in himself content,
Joined them in love's ecstatic sport!

The forest grove by the bank of the Jumna.

Lordly and gay, Nand's dear young Krishna
Sports in the fair forest:
His body's smeared with fresh saffron,
Camphor, and sandal fine,
And sometimes in brake or shaw
From the girls' sight he disappears,
Just as the moon in clouds withdraws—
Plays hide-and-seek with subject stars
That by his light still shine!
From grove to grove he passes, as the moon from cloud to cloud:
As partridges, they gaze with thirsting eyes,
Their longing by their loss intensified!
  And Balbīr led them softly
To the river's charming shore—
To where a grove, by fragrant breezes fanned,
By beauty's fertile hand
Was lavishly adorned;
The air was dim with pollen,
And like a throbbing *vīnā* rang
The bees' sonorous sound!
The *champā's* blossom charmed the heart;
The jasmine's fragrance blew,
The coral-flowers trembled
In a camphor-laden dew:
The cardamoms and cloves
Breathed fresh aroma through the grove,
And amaranths and *ketkīs*
At the mingling perfumes thrilled:
Basils exulted in the scene—
Their fragrance floating in between
Lilies, whose seeds with promise of love's hectic joy are filled!

  And bright and soft the sand—
Most exquisite that strand
Fashioned by Jumna, with her watery hand!

He laughs, thrills to mingling joys,
Touches their breasts, and loins—
Love wakes and burns, unslaked,
As young clouds spill their rain!

The humiliation of Kāmdev.

Now Love appeared, five arrows in his hand;
He'd conquered Brahma, others too,
And came puffed up with pride:
But when he saw young Hari, radiant
Among the young Braj wives,
His heart was stirred with love—
Madan was with his own petard
Hoist high!—He swooned away;
His bow and barbs all scattered lay!
And Passion saw Love's plight,
And beat her breast, afraid:
She clasped the god in her embrace,
Wept nectar-tears upon his face,
Lifted him in her arms,
And fled!

The herdgirls' ecstasy.

And so the girls found Mohan,
So wonderful a being, and so dear!
Truly, they might succumb to pride—
They who were both the herdsmen's brides
And dear to Giridhar!
Their beauty's store, their virtue's hoard
By love's pure bliss are crowned:
Let them exult—Lord Kānha
In love to them is bound!
But only in deep-running streams
Can swirling pools seem fair!
In shallows they're unknown,

Or if they're found, no beauty's theirs:
And so, to fortify their love,
The prince of Braj retired
Some way into the charming grove,
His heart with ardour fired . . .

II

The herdgirls, having been abandoned by Krishna, wander forlorn in the forest. Eventually they meet one of their number, Krishna's favourite, who has also been deserted by him.

If all our food is honey-sweet
Its taste gives no delight!
A bitter tang serves now and then
To whet the appetite:
A coloured cloth when freshly dyed
Seems twice as lovely to the eye—
And at parting for a little while
The fires of love, now banked, blaze bright!
Each instant their eyelids screen
Their eyes from him an aeon seems:
What must they feel when walls divide
Them from him, or the forest hides
His form?
And as a pauper grieves
To find a treasure hoard, but see
It snatched from his hands, so felt the girls
Of Braj, to lose their darling Giridhar!
Lost and forsaken, they implored
The forest trees in their distress,
And vines—ignored their lifelessness!
'Listen, you jasmines all!
And know that Giridhar, our dear,
Has brought us for our profit here—
With our hearts, he's stolen as well
The pride that caused our fall!
You *ketkīs*! has our lover come

This way displeased—the darling son
Of Nand? Perhaps his gentle smile
Has snared your hearts, as well!
And you, who twist begarlanded
With pearl-white flowers—you vines!—
What glimpse of Nand's dear Mohan
Charms those wide-open eyes
Of yours? And you who softly sway
As Balbīr softly filched our hearts away—
Fair coral-tree! Brave oleander! Pray,
Have you seen Krishna in these parts?
Tell us, O sandalwood, where he
Who's dearer than yourself to us may be—
Nand's son, by the world revered?
You soothe men's grief—
Now cool our passions' smart!
We'll ask these flower-decked vines! Can blooms expand
Like theirs, untouched by our fair lover's hand?
Let's follow, friends, and ask these tender hinds
Whose eyes have just seen Hari, so bright they shine!
Kadamba tree! Neem! Mango! why
This silence, for you've seen
Him somewhere, passing by!—
Or you, good orange-tree, or banyan high!'
But when they'd asked
The trees by Jumna's side,
And herbs, they drooped downcast:
What solace lay in words for them, who bore
Such cruelty—and shown on such a shore?
And they cried that earth had spirited away
The butter-thief—the thief of their own hearts—
'He's dear as life to us!
Where is he, pray?
Good *tulsī*! won't you say
To Nanda's Krishna that we're in these straits?—
You whom as Govind's very feet
Each of us venerates!'
And as they wander through the grove
Its thickly-spreading trees

Cast, here and there, dark gloom,
But each fair creature by the moon
Of her own beauty sees:
And now they scour the forest's depths,
Calling as though possessed—
And even act out his capture of their hearts,
By his dear deeds obsessed!
They are the ones who truly see
The worth that in his actions lies—
Who, loving none but Mohan, prize
No more their own identity:
At the fly's sharp sting, the grub lies numb,
Fear-filled—then as a fly is born—
How much the more may love for him
Transform their beings into his own!

And then they found a trace
Of their darling's lovely lotus foot,
Glittering with the imprint
Of wheel, conch, lotus, mace
And Indra's thunderbolt! And now
They reverence the dust he's trod, and set it to their brow—
Dust which the yogis strain
To find within their hearts, but all in vain,
And Shiva, Brahmā too!

But when, nearby,
A rival's tracks—his darling's!—caught their eye,
A-gleaming there, the girls were taken aback,
Looked at each other—followed where they led;
And on ahead one spied
The fresh leaves drawn apart, to form a bower,
Where his dear hands had plaited graceful flowers
Into her hair!
A crystal mirror lay
Gem-studded, lovely there—but without him
Was in despair, and not a word would say
When the Braj girls for news of him enquired:

They pondered on its meaning,
Then one found
A reason for that mirror in those hands
To have been held:
For when the glad lover sat behind her
Plaiting her hair, the joy
Of seeing her beauty would be his no more
Until restored
In that lovely mirror, held in the girl's fair hand—
And there their friend would see *his* noble face!
'Blessed is she!' they cried—
And their hearts were from rancour free!
(Can any jewel crown the heads
Of the selfless saints, but they?)
'Well has she worshipped Hari, the Lord
Most dear, and can afford
To drink his lips' sweet nectar, unafraid!'

And now, a little on ahead,
They saw her stand—the one
For whom their darling, Nand's young lovely son,
With passion burned;
Her pale skin glowed; the light it cast
Shone like a halo on the ground,
As though the earth on which she stood
Had turned to gleaming gold—
Or lightning, flashing from a cloud,
Had struck by her, who'd been so proud,
Or with the moon displeased, his light
Had lingered, when he sank from sight!
Tears flooded from her eyes, ran down
To the earth, drenching her garlands,
And to her face, as to some fragrant flower,
The bees perforce were drawn!
And she stands alone, and cries
'Dear lord whose arm is long
To save the ones you love, what has become
Of you? Where have you gone?
Birds, beasts repine—the very vines

Weep, as I cry forlorn!'
  They ran and took her in their arms;
Each held her to her breast—
They'd lost love's richest prize,
But found in her a second best,
And led her back towards the Jumna's shore
Where Nand's dear son had sported,
He whom the world adores . . .

III

The girls complain that Krishna has still not reappeared, and at the same time are moved with compassion for him.

'Young Kānha!' they exclaim,
'Since first you came to Braj, fickle Indirā
Has prospered, well arrayed—
And here has stayed!
Why strike this cruel stroke, and hide away?
Why slay us with your smile, lord of love's sport?—
Though we're your slaves, no price for us you've paid!
Why keep us safe from flood and flame
For this, good Kānha, and from serpent's bane?
Why with Govardhan shield us, when
The lightning fell like rain—not let us die?
Dearest, be not so vain
That from Yashodā you took birth,
For the entreaty brought you forth
That we to Brahmā made,
That you might save the universe!
O ruler of our lives! O friend!
If you strike down
The ones who are your own
There's nothing, surely, you'd defend!
When in the wood
You set your gentle feet, the herds to tend,
Our hearts are by its thorns
And rocks, stones, grasses torn;
How fitting, if these hearts were now restored,

Dear lord,
By their lotus touch, which are
Devotion's cynosure!
Good Kānha, if unterrified
Your feet on Kāliya's hoods you placed,
Then lay them at our curving breasts
Now, and be not afraid!

Dear king of Braj, we know now what you fear:
Your feet are lotus-soft, our nipples firm!
Set them down softly, love, those feet so dear;
How far they've wandered in the wood, by many a sharp
    spine torn!'

IV

Krishna now reappears; the girls' delight and devotion, as they gather round him; Krishna is moved by their love.

And the waves rose upon their love's sweet sea!
Their young hearts tossed, and to their darling they
Called waywardly—
                                        and now good Giridhar
Was there among them! Like a conjurer
Who's seemed to vanish, now he reappears:
With yellow robe, and garland
Of wild flowers, and in his hand
His slender flute, he smiles that tender smile
That stirs the lovegod with love's passion wild!
And seeing their beloved
The troop of girls leapt to their feet, as one,
Just as their senses at his sight had flamed—
Just as new life had to their bodies come!
And none who starve so madly crave
Food, as for him they long;
No mortal hunger theirs, their love
Ten million times more strong!

One quickly clutched his hand; one clung

To his darling breast; another hung
At his cheek, and scolded her false Kānha dear;
One in both hands held fast his robe—
And crisscross lightning framed the cloud
Fresh-gathered, that was their good Giridhar!
And on that bank they sat,
And perfect bliss was theirs!
The girls spread out their clothes—a sight
As fine as they themselves were fair—
And now each found that on the ground
Lord Hari sat with her alone,
To satisfy her longing
As she might most desire!
This is the way that mighty yogis
Fasten within their hearts
One form, all at one time—and all
Attain to joy, as their deserts;
And though the dark god rules
Uncounted cosmoses as his alone,
It's they, the assembled queens of Braj,
Who truly grace his throne!
He shone like a king, fair Shyām,
Among those lovely ones,
Just as a lotus seed-pod, ringed
By its fresh petals, gleams;
And smiling in their hearts
The young girls asked their dear Nandlāl love's ways—
  'Now Kānha, say:
  Some worship you with love, and some
  May love, whose way of love's unknown;
  If these two paths are only one
  How else may love be shown?'
And he, beloved of Nanda,
The mentor of the world,
Good Giridhar, the prince of Braj,
Was to those girls by love so bound
That no reply he found!
And when words came he said 'How much I owe
To you girls!

You should put me far from your hearts, for the fault is mine!
My heart is yours—and know
That ages without end spent serving you
Were all too few
To pay the debt I owe!
What if my power, that spreads the universe,
So splendid seems?
Yours is in love, and by this I myself
Am charmed!'

V

The dance with Krishna, and Nanddās's epilogue.

They heard their darling's words of love; in each her anger died,
And laughing, they embrace him—and in the lotus shade
Of his feet ten million wishing trees shine, and their fragrance shed,
And cows of plenty many a one roll in the dust he treads!
And when he smiled, the herdgirls knew
His like had never been—
The root of timeless joy,
To draw from each heart its pain:

And now the dance began!
Miraculous it was, on the magic disc
Of that same lotus, that now held their weight
As they danced, in their colours bright:
And the emerald glow, and golden gleam
As his beauty mingled with theirs, now seemed
A necklace laid at Vrindāvan's throat,
And the girls, and young Shyām, her delight!
His flute's sweet sound, and their clapping hands,
Anklets and bracelets and belts a-jingle,
Cymbals and lutes, and drums of all kinds,
In one abandon mingle;

The tambourines clash, the strings resound,
And bees drone low to a pipe's clear sound
While the *vīnās* ring, and their soft feet spring,
And fine earrings and garlands glitter and swing!
Gaily the Braj girls danced with their dark lover,
Flashed like a wreath of lightning, laid round
Some towering, lovely cloud;
And tossing braids
Swung out behind the graceful girls like lines
Of bees, that trail from Beauty's swinging vines!
May their dear Mohan's loving arts—
The peacock-feather swaying on his crown,
The saffron of his flapping gown—
Dwell always in my heart!
And as one reached out for another's hand
While she danced, her twirling palm
Seemed to spin like a top—set the lover's heart
A-reel in delight at her charms!
A third, by *his* charms enslaved,
Mimicked the secret signs he gave
Of his love, as she sang his praise:
And their good Nandlāl was amazed at the sight,
As a child sees his face in a glass, and is lost in delight!
All share the same joy,
And they throw off their jewels as offerings to him,
And the clothes from their bodies, but others fly
Straightway to replace them, bright
With a transcendental light!
One adds her gay voice to the flute and the noise of the
    throng,
And another outsings the flute, so divine her song!
And with a laugh their dark young lord
Catches her, delighted, in his arms,
Kisses the mouth in which that song was born,
Stains it with *pān*, that from his own has run:
For the music and dance that charms gods and men
    in this world
Is inborn in the girls
Of Braj, and their song

In the sacred texts is sung!
What mortal poet finds words
To tell the delight of that glorious round-dance
Danced by those girls divine?
And who can describe their song
Whose very speech rings with the harmony
Of *rāg* and *rāginī*? Or the way they hang
About him as they dance, can this be told?—
Their arms about his neck, his about theirs,
Adding to love's delight with joy newfold!

And so the dance went on:
Its charm not of this world—for its sound and song
Has power to melt the sages' hearts, transform
Stones into running streams, and streams to stone;
And the wind died, and the moon grew tired
On his path, and the firmament stood still;
The sun's car lagged in his course behind
As the autumn night drew out, a-thrill
To see those dear girls and Shyām delight
In love's passion, as long as was their will!
How many joys they knew in that glad grove—
Their home! and when to Jumna's stream
They went to frolic, how many gods of love
Might blush with shame
To see the garlands crushed upon their breasts,
To think the thought their wanton gait suggests—
Those eyes, as delighted they rove,
Those foreheads, shining with bright beads of sweat!
And now they plunge in Jumna's stream,
Brighter in beauty than a man can say,
And gambol, as an elephant-king may
Among his tender queens;
Their bodies lie unseen,
But their lovely faces float! and gleam
Brightly like golden lotuses
On Jumna's waves—
And now they splash him gracefully
With water, cupping hands: so may

The lotus-cluster splash, in play,
The bee with nectar-spray!

This dance, and its joy divine,
Are beyond our power to tell—
Shesha may sing it, but his thousand tongues
Still labour at the tale;
Shiva may hold it in his heart
But of it tells no part,
And Sanaka, Sanandan, Shārdā,
And Nārada delighted on it dwell:
The birthless god for fair Vrindāvan's dust
Still longs, and finds no grain—
His heart impaled upon this stake of pain;
The lotus goddess tends
His lotus feet by night and day, unstained,
But never, even in dreams, has she
Such joy attained,
For only those whose right it is
May see Vrindāvan! How can others hope
To see its dust, who still towards it grope?
And as the soul, that guides our hearts,
Dwells here within the flesh, unfound
By the senses in their passions blind,
So hides Vrindāvan from our sight!

The man who sings these deeds
Or hears them sung, and tells with care again,
Will find true love, God's grace,
And honour from all men;
But let him not tell the tale
To infidels, and those whose trust is small,
To slanderers, and those beyond the pale
Of Hari's love—if so, no joy he'll win:
Let the devoted hear it, they
Whose strength is in the Bhāgvat faith,
Like Jumna's fish, that never stray
Beyond her waves' embrace—
For though the seven seas receive

Her waters, as the Vedas say,
All streams they shun, save hers alone,
And still in Jumna's play!

I've strung this glowing garland
Of delight with pains untold;
Let him take care, who would it wear—
Nor snap the thread that holds
These choicest blossoms, culled from tales to hear,
From songs to sing, and calling on his name,
From knowledge, thought for Hari, and the Vedas too,
I claim!
They vanquish sin, and charm the heart;
Love in its beauty they bestow;
Now may they rest on Nanddās' breast,
Always to bring him joy!

UDDHAV'S MESSAGE

Uddhav has arrived from the city of Mathura with a message from Krishna, and addresses the herdgirls, who have been longing for him in his absence.

'Attend to Uddhav,
Good women of Braj!
In you all gifts dwell—beauty,
Virtue, charm;
You flaunt love's banner, and give form
To love's delight, awakening rich joy,
And sport with the fair one, Shyām,
In Vrindāvan's fresh groves,
Good women of Braj!

I bring a message from Shyām,
But no chance have I found to set a time
To give it to you;
Always I ponder
When we might meet, and when I might return
To Mathura city,
With Nandlāl's message given,
Women of Braj!'

They heard Shyām's name—
And thoughts of home and village fled, bliss filled
Their hearts;
The vine of their love flowered, clinging to its tree!
Tears welled to their eyes; their bodies thrilled
In shivering delight,
And throats
Tightened in stammered, wordless ecstasy,
As is love's way:

He sat, and round their honoured guest
They filed in proper welcome—
Urged their attentions on him, for they knew
Shyām's friend was among them here!
Joyful of face
They asked news of Nandlāl, these young Braj girls,
Declaring sweetly 'Kind is our Balbīr,
O friend of Shyām.'

'Shyām and Balrām, and all their retinue
Are well, and all the Yadu kin—
All flourish! And to learn
How Braj has prospered, here on this bank
I come to you;
Grieve not,
He'll soon return,
Women of Braj!'

The girls faint at the thought of Krishna. Uddhav tries to console them with his abstract view of Krishna as the omnipresent, impersonal brahman. *The girls reject this view indignantly, seeing Krishna as a supreme being of personal attributes, attainable not by yoga but by love* (bhakti). *Uddhav and the girls speak in alternate stanzas in this section of the poem, and the girls have the last word.*

These words from Mohan brought his image dear
Back to their minds—
And through their lips, their hair
An ecstatic shiver ran, betrayed
Their bodies' frenzy!
Racked and faint,
They fell to the ground, these women: Uddhav
Splashed them with water, rousing them with the words
'Women of Braj!—

He's near you—look, and truly know!
In the whole teeming cosmos, every form
Is Brahma,
Discrete though it may be:
Metal and stone,
Wood, water, earth and sky, all things
Quick or inert, reflect as their own light
Brahma's radiance,
Women of Braj!'

'What light of Brahma? Who are we to hear
Of knowledge, Uddhav?
Shyām the fair is ours!
Our path of love is straight—Mohan reveals
In eye, ear, nostril, voice
His form so dear,
Snatching our minds and memories with his flute—
Casting love's spell,
O friend of Shyām!'

'But all these things are attributes
Of the conditioned world! His form
Is unconditioned, changeless, unattached
To the three qualities!
No hands nor feet are his,
Nor nostril, eye, nor voice nor ear,
For the light cast by the undying Krishna
Is Brahma's radiance, breath of all being,
Women of Braj!'

'Had he no mouth?
Then say, who ate the butter?
No feet?
Then say who ran from grove to grove
Following the cows? He smeared collyrium
Below his eyes, and lifted in his hand
Govardhan hill, known as Yashodā's son
And Nand's—
Young Kānha, lord of Braj,
—O friend of Shyām!'

'You call him Kānha—he who's fatherless,
Nor born of mother!—and from whom arose
The universe entire,
The egg of Brahmā!
He took man's shape, and came to earth
To work his will, as Shyām;
But yoga's discipline alone wins him,
And highest Brahma's city is his home,
O women of Braj!'

'Tell *him* of yoga, Uddhav, whom you find
Fit for it,
But to us sing lovingly
Of Nanda-nandana's reality!
In Mohan's eye the proof of his being shines!
It fills his voice, heart, soul—
And where's the man
Who scorns love's nectar, turning to scoop up dust,
O friend of Shyām?'

'Is dust so worthless? Why does dust besmear
Shiv's sacred head—the lord's
Who came into this world of dust
Through *karma's* law, as Hari?
From dust alone this frame was formed, from dust
The egg of Brahmā,
And the fourteen worlds, seven isles,
Nine continents,
Women of Braj!'

'*Karm* and the like
Are known to those who claim it for themselves—
Who defile love's nectar with its dust!
Karm holds full sway
Only while Hari's absent from the heart,
And each created being in its bonds
In vain travails,
O friend of Shyām!'

'Why slander *karm*? Thence springs
Well-being,
And the three worlds hold
No mightier power;
It's *karm* that brings to birth,
Karm that destroys, and acts under its law
Win release,
Repose in Brahma's realm,
O women of Braj!'

'*Karma* is action both for good, and ill!
A fetter forged of gold, but iron as well;
For the feet twin shackles—prize them if you will!
High *karma* leads to heaven, low to the hell
Of sensuality—but even so
All die, by lust's canker gnawn,
If love they've never known,
O friend of Shyām!'

'If *karma's* worthless, why do men embrace
Yoga?—
Why seal the body's doors, repress
The senses, sitting in the lotus pose?
And purged in Brahma's fire,
Why seek the trance
That leads to absorption in the absolute,
Merging of light in light,
O women of Braj?'

'The yogis worship light, but devotees
Find in their god a personality!
They take Shyāmsundar to their heart
As the nectar of love, revealed—
For behind the qualified how few have thought
That an absolute's concealed!
Just so, when a snake inside a house has slid,
Men worship at the hole where it is hid,
O friend of Shyām!'

'Shyām has no qualities! The Vedas state
Their negative, and Upanishads propound
The Self as absolute,
Though seeming qualified!
Vedas, Puranas too have never found
One quality; if all is qualified,
Say, what supports the sky,
O women of Braj?'

'Has Shyām no qualities? Then how
Are qualities formed, we'd like to know!
How can a tree unseeded grow?
His quality, though single,
In illusion's mirror gleams
Reflected, and many seems:
So pure and muddy streams
—Both water—mingle,
O friend of Shyām!'

‘Remember, though, that Hari’s qualities
Are not those shown by error! Why
Confuse these two?
That Being’s mystery
Eludes the Vedas and Upanishads
Even when they grasp its quality and form;
And so they name it Brahma the unqualified,
O women of Braj!’

‘The Vedas? They’re the breath he breathes—
Forms of his too, though no one sees
This truth, engrossed in acts and ritual!
Through acts all seek him, but not one
Glimpses his form—while they who shun
Action attain him—they alone!
In this love’s special power is shown,
O friend of Shyām!’

‘Love is a craving for an object seen
And felt as real; what lover ever yearns
For love unseen, unreal?
None have divined
The qualities that lend the sun and moon
Their forms—what of that Being then, the lord
Beyond all qualities,
O women of Braj?’

‘The sun is heaven’s light—its form
In its own splendour lies concealed:
Only to him who sees aright
Is divine reality revealed!
And why should those without such sight
See Hari’s form, we ask?
And why feel faith awakening
Who into the pit of *karm* are cast,
O friend of Shyām?’

'The round of *karma* gives devotion too
Its place—but who's exempt
From *karma's* process?
Karma is annulled
Only by acts, performed unfailingly
Under its law; then the Self, freed from *karma*,
Merges in Brahma, the Unqualified,
O women of Braj.'

'*Karm*'s a vain bond, if Hari's free
Of *karm*—and your 'Unqualified'
We'd call mere substance—just a key
Conferring knowledge! But if he
By such means is identified
He's not supreme—this can't be so!
The ultimate's conditioned, we know,
For the whole world is qualified,
O friend of Shyām!'

'All qualities apparent to the eye
Must vanish, but eternal Vāsudev
Suffers no taint from these!
His radiance
Is that of perfect knowledge—undisclosed
To the gross senses, seen by those
Who know this truth of him, the babe reborn,
O women of Braj.'

'Can disbelievers recognise
That form beneficent? They spurn
The sun itself, in yonder skies,
And to clutch at its scattered rays they turn!
But we're intent upon that form
And countless Brahmas no more prize
Than a tiny plum, that lies
Unseen within the palm—
O friend of Shyām!'

The girls are now carried away in an ecstasy of longing. One by one they reproach Krishna for his indifference to them, and for his harshness, especially to women, in earlier avatārs.

And now, before their eyes,
A vision of Nandlāl arose:
To pledge his love he stands there, radiant
In marriage robes!
They turn to *him* from Uddhav,
And in their speech love's nectar flows,
From their lotus eyes tears fall,
Proving their way of love:

'O lord of Lakshmī and the Yadus, lord
Of man and beast, the anxious cattle stray
Abandoned through the woods,
Nand-nandana!
Relent, return, remembering your herds
And herdsmen, for we sink
Into a sea of grief; hold out your hand
To save us, cruel one—
Where have you been?'

'Reveal yourself,' one begged, 'and sound your flute!
Why linger far off, beyond the forest's screen?
Why sear our longing hearts?
In you alone
We, and uncounted millions, find
Our love's dear cynosure; do not requite
Such love by breaking off your own—
Never, dear Krishna!'

And one complained 'You show yourself,
Then vanish!
Say, dear, who taught you this deceit?
We live by joy of love alone,
So all speak sadly now—what hope of life
Fills the caught fish, that's from the water drawn?
Think of this, Krishna!'

A third enquired
'Can this be upstart pride?
With Mathura in your power, O Shyām,
You act the emperor—
But all can see
What price to lay upon your sovereignty!
The world's kings well may tremble, to be told
You've struck down helpless women—
O king so bold!'

And one said 'Shyām, it seems you're bent
On slaying us—how was it then
You held Govardhan's mountain-tent
Above us?—from the fiery bane
Of Kāliya, and forest's flame
Preserved us always—to torment
Us now with longing's fire, young laughing Nand,
And steal away our minds?'

One said 'He's merciless—and free
From fault! Both sin and merit rest
Within his gift, and what can we
Expect from him but cruelty,
When, still a babe, from Pūtanā's breast
He sucked the milk, and life away:
Whose friend is he?'

One said 'We've seen this cruelty
Before now in Rāmchandra too—
His acts, his bearing—are they new?
Why, he, that light of Raghu's race,
Slew Tārakā the demoness
While on his way
To guarantee
The sage's sacrifice
—Though still a boy!'

'He's the high Law,' another said,
—'Though wed to a woman's will!
A warrior, whose weapon turns
To each new target he discerns:
When he learned from Sītā of Shūrpnakhā
What anger on her fell!
Her face was slashed, her figure marred,
For honour or disgrace none cared—
How sad her tale!'

'And that's not all, my dear,' another said.
'You know he went, flower-decked,
To beg three steps of land from Bali the king?
As a dwarf he addressed him,
Then took a form
Mountainous, incorporeal—set foot
On Bali's back, of bounden duty heedless—
High priest of greed!'

And one exclaimed 'How could the brash Prahlād
Take umbrage at King Hiranyakashipu—
Feud with his father,
Who decreed,
To instruct the lad, a proper penalty:
But Krishna in Man-lion's form burst free
To rend him with his claws
—Quite without cause!'

'When born as Parashurām,' one said,
'With axe on shoulder laid,
He struck his mother down, swept clear
The earth of *kshatriyas*—revered
His fathers in a sacrifice
Standing in pools of blood; should he
Intend for us no cruelty?
From him, can ill-will alone suffice?'

And one said 'Why, what harm was planned
By Shishupāl the king, who went
To marry in King Bhīshmak's land—
Stood splendid, and intent
Amid his retinue's assembled might
To guard his bride?
But Krishna duped him, stole her off,
Snatched the fair morsel from his famished mouth,
Driven on by greed!'

Uddhav is moved by the girls' anguish. He now sees the rightness of their point of view, and longs for their favour.

And so by a frenzy
The herdgirls were possessed:
They craved his love divine, and now
Dwelt upon forms and actions new
Of the beloved!
What doubt is there
That they, in whose bodies' every pore
Mohan abides, have knowledge pure
Of past and future,
By their love obsessed?

When Uddhav saw their love, his level mood
Deserted him! A fit of gloom and shame
Oppressed his heart,
And in his heart he saw
That the dust of their feet, when on the forehead laid,
Gains one life's highest goal—love's bliss
In the three worlds: 'These women
One must adore!'

And he thought 'If I can sing
Shyām's praises, and delight them,
Loving devotion surely will be mine
To Shyām the fair!
To please them I'll do all I can,
And then my heart, once purified,
Will set at rest the doubts that rise
From knowledge, and will win
Love's joy!'

A bee flies past; the girls project upon it their resentment of Uddhav and his arguments (and also of Krishna's treatment of them). They burst into tears. Uddhav has by now come to feel such devotion for them that he is more than ready to renounce his earlier views. Finally he returns to Mathura. Krishna, contrite at his news, grants him a vision of himself in the form of a herdgirl, and vanishes.

Just then a bee, that chanced to fly that way,
Came humming, bright in beauty, through the throng
Of the Braj women,
And on their feet
(Thinking the nails red lotuses) went to alight:
The girls were startled by its sudden flight!
And saw in it a metamorphosis
Into bee's form
Of Uddhav!

And to that bee
Each one now made her own reply—
Of words a subtle snare
Instinct with love's delight, but linked to sense:
'Don't touch my feet! Away!
You filch the joy
And bliss we feel, and Mohan, that dear boy,
Deceived us, just as you—
Be off! Fly hence!'

'Why, everything born black,' said one,
'Is devious, guileful, cruel—and if a man
The darkest villain!
We know this—our limbs
Touched his dark body, and to this day burn!
And now this bee comes here, and brings
The serpent yoga, with its sting!
He'll have no mercy!'

'This bee looks like *him*!' one exclaimed,
'Black body, yellow-swathed;
Girdle a-tinkling, ringing voice!
Now back to Braj a path he's traced
With pilfered curd, from yonder place
Of his—don't trust him anyone, beware
That shape so sly! Be sure
That everything is here!'

One cried 'You're called a lover, bee,
But why, for what ability?
This baffles us! We only see
Black body, yellow face,
Proclaiming sin, and your disgrace
In the world's eyes!
Then recognise
Your sum of virtue, bee, and vice—
Look in a glass!'

And one asked 'Can a bee
Be schooled in love's delight?
On many a flower you light,
But each one as yourself you see,
And seek malignly to awake in us
The doubts you revel in—make rancorous
Our bliss of love
With sly duplicity!'

One said 'Why bee,
Can *you* sing Mohan's praises?
Can the finest love flower in a furtive heart?
You know what Hari's like—in him you've stolen
All that we have,
And here among the young Braj wives
Will any trust you?
Rightly we've given him love!'

'You sip the flowers,' one said,
'But who'd agree you make one drop of honey?
You fly, murmuring of yoga, mortal snare
For one in love;
You've tasted blood at many a lip,
And dyed its rose to red—
What brings you here to Braj, whom will you slay now?
Away, sinful one!'

And one said, 'Tell me, bee,
What creature like yourself—six-legged and dull of wit—
Ever knew love?
We've seen none such till now in this land of Braj!
—But horned like brute beasts,
Black-bodied, striped with yellow,
You lick stale lees for nectar, and take fright
At the true nectar's sight;
Your love's all wind and words!'

Another said, 'Why, bee, this teaching's vain!
Why peddle *karm* to love's disciples—we've risen
Above wishing release!
To those who cling
To Mohan's being, the core
Of Vedas and Puranas, why preach your lore
Of reaching the true Self—
In yoga's school?'

And one said 'Look, you're skilled
In existential argument, and find
Support in logic, and the scriptures too
A-plenty—but to this you're blind,
That no reality's unqualified,
And in Shyām's unconditioned power
Condition's found,
As a bubble shines, light-filled!'

One said 'Have you no shame?
Your master's Shyām—he's called the hunchback's lover,
And never would deign to come here
To love us cowherd girls!
—Of course, to eat scraps left by his concubine
Must sanctify the Yadus—
Don't you think so?
Don't speak to us!'

And one said 'Look, if Shyām's a yogi,
You're his disciple then!
Turn to the hunchback—make her your pilgrimage,
Make sensuality your fair!
You've peddled talk of final liberation
All over Mathura,
But love's the rule in Gokul,
Who'll want your ware?
Be off, sir!'

Another said 'Look, bee, if Mathura's holy men
Are like yourself, what of its sages then?
You twist vice into virtue, but deform
Virtue itself:
And surely Mohan would flee this body's form
On sight of saints like you—
Squander his wealth!'

'Are all your friends like this?' said one;
'If so, we understand
Why he of the dark body should dissemble
On every hand!
In Gokul here
Murāri, though a lover, found no mate,
But matched to his own bent limbs
A hunchbacked mistress,
Twisted in form and ways!'

And in this way
Each herdgirl addressed Uddhav as the bee,
Filled with the longing of Govinda's Lay,
Unmindful of becoming modesty!
Then all at once
All these Braj women wept,
Crying 'Lord, show pity!
Keshav—Krishna—Murāri!
Our hearts are rent!'

And from their eyes there streamed
A flood of tears, that swelled and drowned
Its lotus sources—drenching
Bodices, garlands, necklaces;
—While in that sea of love
Uddhav, who'd come to Braj to dike it round
With knowledge, was swept off,
And his race redeemed!

Now he praised their love,
And declared a pure devotion, that swept away
All knowledge, dogged by doubt,
All dullness, passivity!
And this Uddhav was heard to say
—Fit vessel now for the draught of Hari's love—
That the sight of those girls was enough
To win him life's goal,
Wash knowledge's taint away!

Time and again he declared 'Hari sent me
Out to this lonely place
To speak to them, but of their secret I learned
Nothing, and found no trace;
The views I thought right, I advised,
Of knowledge and action I spoke,
But all of them cling to their love, despise
The conventional ways of their folk!
God bless these herdgirls!

And surely they will attain
To joy's height, and the station of love
Who flee to Mohan, disdain
Like them, a conventional life!
Knowledge and yoga—such things
Spring from *karm*, but are truly surpassed
By love; alongside diamonds
I'll not rank glass!
What madness is this?

Blessed, twice blessed
Are they who adore Hari so!
And how may others find love
Without him, love's touchstone? Pride
At this little learning of mine barred my path,
Filled my heart,
Till I learned that of love as you know it learning was worth
No more than a tiny part:
In vain men have toiled and died!'

Then he said 'My friends,
The best of all things is communion with the good,
A touchstone, to transmute
Base iron to gold;
The leavings from these herdgirls' offering
Of love are mine to savour:
I, Uddhav, spurn
Knowledge and doubt, and like a bee I turn
To love, and its nectar's flavour!'

And he touched their feet—
Cried that they first from error's way had turned him;
A bee they had named him! Spurned him
As one in disgrace most deep!
'Now let me lie like dust on the paths of this place
To be touched by their feet as they pass,
The source of life
And all happiness,
But how hard to find for a sage!

Or let me be found as a creeper, or vine, or brake
In the wood,
Where their shadow upon me may fall
As they wander at will!
It's not in my power to decide the form I shall take,
But to Mohan I'll go—
With his favour I'll beg this boon;
May he grant it be done!'

And now his heart filled
With this wish, and his body thrilled
In tremulous, mute delight, and he took his way back
To Mathura.
And Mohan's qualities he quite forgot!
And the herdgirls' virtues now began to sing,
Rejecting life—in them discovering
The root of life itself—
Devotion's heart!

So thinking, to Shyām he sped,
Prostrated himself, turned about him,
Spoke much of his love, and said
That the women of Braj knew love's ways—
Though Shyām might flout them!
And his eyes
Flashed in anger—but joy filled his voice:
'O darling of Nand!—

Your love, with its pity and joy,
Is all a lie;
Its worth is untold
While its prospect before us you hold,
But I've been to Braj, I've learned of your cruelty:
You're ready to cast into damnation's well
Those girls, who upon you rely!
What justice is this?

Return, remain in Vrindāvan, I beg you!
Enjoy with those herdgirls the riches of perfect love!
Turn aside from all other tasks,
Bring them joy,
Uddhav asks,
Or their love and affection will fail straightway—
Will be gone!
Shall it be done?'

When he heard these words from his friend
Tears sprang to his eyes,
And memory fled, constrained
In passion's ecstasy!
Each hair of the dark body thrilled, instinct
With a herdgirl's being,
As if the Braj girls were the leaves of some dark wishing-tree,
—From his whole body springing!

Then his senses returned, and he said 'It was well that I sent you there
To remind them, friend, of myself,
For now you've returned, I find,
To tell me wherein *I* err!
But between myself and them I draw no line—
Not of any sort, not ever at any time,
And as they are found in me, so I in them—
So waves from water form!'

And all at once, the flowerdecked god appeared
To Uddhav as a herdgirl—
Put an end to error, rent
Illusion's veil!
Then taking his own form, he passed
From sight; and now Nanddās
Is purified, having sung the splendid tale
Of Krishna's deeds—
Rich in love's sweet content!

NOTES

Rāspancādhyāyī

l. 1 Śuka: Son of the legendary 'great sage' (*maharṣi*) Vyāsa, the supposed composer of the *Bhāgavata Purāṇa*. Śuka is said to have recited the *Purāṇa* to the sages and kings of mankind, including King Parīkṣit, whose salvation this brought about. He is described in the *Purāṇa* as an *avadhūta*, one who has discarded worldly obligations, and his wanderings through the world in which he stops only briefly in any one place are mentioned. Nanddās uses the word *naga* 'immovable object' which often means 'mountain', sometimes 'tree, plant', to describe the obstacles in his way. The *Purāṇa's* account provides or suggests most of the details of Nanddās's description of Śuka.

4 Hari: A common name of Vishnu-Krishna.

26 his namesake's shape and sheen: A play on the literal meaning 'parrot' of the word *śuka*.

27 At his throat, voluted lines . . .: The expression *kambukaṇṭha* 'shellneck' of the original refers to the presence of auspicious marks or lines on the neck, suggestive of the curves of a conch shell; the latter is one of the emblems of Vishnu, and itself an auspicious object.

33 Kānha: A common form of the name Krishna, especially as applied to Gopāl Krishna, the cowherd god.

37 delight: The delight or *rasa* in Krishna that arises in Śuka's heart is imagined in physical terms, as flowing down to what Śrīdhar, a commentator on the *Purāṇa*, calls the 'whirlpool shape' of his navel. Implicit in the imagery here is the notion of the navel as one of the sources of life, which is given Vaishnava form in the story of the god Brahmā's birth from a lotus springing from Vishnu's navel.

42 the arms reach to the knees: *ājānu bāhu*. With this attribute of Śuka, drawn from the *Bhāgavata Purāṇa* (I. 19. 27), may be compared Krishna's title *mahābāhu* 'long-armed', referred to in the *Mahābhārata* (V. 2567) and also by Nanddās in this poem (translation, l. 546).

54 five chapters: *Bhāgavata Purāṇa* X. 29–33.

58 a friend's request: Apart from the *Rāspancādhyāyī*, Nanddās's *Dasamskandh* and *Rasmanjarī* also mention a 'friend' at whose instance they are said to have been composed, and attempts have been made to identify this supposed friend

in the light of statements in the *vārtās*, and in his *Rūpmanjarī*. These attempts seem quite conjectural, and despite some circumstantial detail in the *Rasmanjarī* references it is likely that the 'friend' merely provides a conventional explanation for Nanddās's undertaking some of his adaptations from Sanskrit sources.

58 who lives for Krishna's love alone: *parama rasika* 'supremely *rasik*'; one who finds perfect fulfilment only in experiencing the *rasa*, or savour, of passionate love for Krishna. Krishna, too, is himself a *rasik*, finding this same *rasa* in communion with his devotees. The notions of *rasa* and of passionate love as an expression of love for the divine are referred to above, pp. 44 f.

62 Vṛndāvan: To Nanddās and the Vallabhans there exists a celestial Vṛndāvan which is Krishna's highest heaven, *cidghana* 'composed of thought', not *prākṛta* 'material', and dependent on his *aiśvarya;* this is his Goloka, where the most perfect of his devotees sport with him forever. The earthly Vṛndāvan is no more than pale reflection of this realm.

70 bonds of time and quality: The celestial Vṛndāvan is beyond both time and the material qualities or *guṇas* of which the phenomenal world is composed.

79 Lakṣmī: Vishnu's consort and the goddess of good fortune. Other names of hers which are used in this poem are Ramā, Kamalā and Indirā. Prosperity is the result of fickle Lakṣmī's consenting to stay temporarily among her devotees; similarly Nanddās says here that Lakṣmī endows the forests of earth with whatever natural riches she pleases, not with the entire beauty of her *svarūpa*, her proper divine form or entity, in which she attends Vishnu-Krishna as his consort. (Krishna's consort is, strictly speaking, Rukmiṇī rather than Lakṣmī according to the *Bhāgavata Purāṇa*).

86 Saṅkarṣaṇ: This name originally refers to one of four manifestations of the god Vāsudeva according to certain early theistic belief. Later Vaishnavism identifies Saṅkarṣaṇ with Gopāl Krishna's elder brother, Balrām.

87 Ramā: See note to Lakṣmī, l. 79.

88 Nārāyaṇ: 'the son of *nara*', i.e. of man; a name of the supreme being going back to very early tradition. Nārāyaṇ's

identity merges with that of the Bhāgavata deity, and hence the name refers very often to Vishnu or Krishna.

94 the very gods of poetry: The reference is essentially to the mythological serpent Śeṣa, on whose coils Vishnu is said to rest during periods of inactivity and whose thousand tongues, says Nanddās, are not enough to describe Vṛndāvan; with Śeṣa are linked the rhyming names Maheśa (Śiva), Gaṇeśa (the god of wisdom and remover of obstacles in any undertaking) and Sureśa (the Vedic god Indra; the name also refers to Vishnu-Krishna).

98 Indra's wishing-tree: The *kalpataru*, one of the trees of Indra's heaven, supposed to grant all desires (like the *cintāmaṇi* or 'jewel of thought', also mentioned by Nanddās here). *Bhāgavata Purāṇa* X. 38. 22 compares Krishna to Indra's wishing-tree, as granting all his devotees' desires.

100 glittering gems: The opulence of the celestial Vṛndāvan, as described by Nanddās, is suggestive of relatively late *śākta* treatments of the Krishna theme which emphasise the importance of Rādhā, such as the *Brahmavaivarta Purāṇa* and the Rādhā-Vallabha sect of Harivaṃśa (16th century). It is of interest that Harivaṃśa's Sanskrit *Rādhāsudhānidhi* opens with an invocation to Vṛndāvan; although the main impetus to Nanddās's including a separate account of Vṛndāvan in this poem probably comes rather from earlier traditions, e.g. as taken up by Sūrdās, see ed. cit., *pada* 1973, and pp. 40 f. above. See also note to l. 508 of the translation.

104 nymphs: *apsarases*, a class of female deities, wives of heaven-dwelling musicians or singers known as Gandharvas.

104 minstrels: Gandharvas and *kinnaras*, a section of the Gandharvas in later mythology.

117 dais: By this is meant a circular raised area of ground, the area of the *rās* dance, in which the herdgirls dance in a circle around Krishna (or Krishna and Rādhā). The sixteen petals of the lotus growing from the dais symbolise its perfection (though the number sixteen is a stock one in descriptions and enumerations). Nanddās makes this divine lotus itself the actual site of the soul's supernatural dance with Krishna (translation, ll. 668 ff.).

124 mighty prince of lovers: *vara rasika purandara* 'choice *rasik*, Purandar'. See note to l. 59 for the word *rasika*. The title *Purandara* 'city-destroyer' is applied usually to the Vedic

god Indra; Indra 'Purandara' is in the *Ṛg Veda* the destroyer of the settlements of the Dāsas, the pre-Indo-Aryan inhabitants of north India, and the slayer of the demon Vṛtra (in which act he was assisted by Vishnu). The title is also applied to Vishnu, in which use it reflects this early connection of Vishnu with Indra, as well as the later upgrading of Vishnu-Krishna at the expense of earlier deities, and hostility between Krishna and Indra (e.g., see note to l. 300). These relationships are again evident in the symbolism of the thunderbolt as used by Nanddās later in this poem (translation, l. 495), and in other occasional references.

125 jewel: Referred to by its name, *kaustubha,* in the text. Originally a symbol of fertility, see Gonda, *Aspects of Early Viṣṇuism,* p. 100.

129 Mohan: 'the infatuating one'; a name of Krishna symbolising the personal and *saguṇa* elements of his divine nature (of which Nanddās is here saying that the impersonal *brahman* is only an aspect).

132 guides the beating of each heart: Krishna is the *antaryāmī* or 'internal controller' of the soul. See p. 22.

133 universal soul: *paramātmā* 'supreme self', i.e. the supreme being; see Introduction, p. 9.

133 high spirit: *parabrahma* 'the supreme *brahman*'; see Introduction, p. 9.

134 primeval god: Nārāyaṇ; see note to l. 88.

135 blessed one: *Bhagavān,* the supreme lord Vishnu-Krishna as worshipped with devotion; this title and the word *bhakti* share the same root.

135 righteous: The sense is 'in accordance with *dharma*', which means here the divine law or ordinance of creation. In the next line and later in this chapter the word is used again in the same sense, while in two occurrences at the end of the poem it has rather the senses 'religious faith' or even 'way of life, obligations of a believer'. From the point of view of a devout Hindu the word comprises the whole complex of religious and social obligations which it is one's duty to meet in life, and the grace deriving from their fulfilment.

143 Vishnu's paradise: *Vaikuṇṭha,* a high realm, but far inferior to Krishna's *Goloka.* It is above all Krishna's deeds,

Nanddās tells us in this passage, that throw light on the nature of the divine law (*dharma*).

165 red powder: The substance known as *gulāl* (the word used by Nanddās here), often ground stone, coloured with a red dye, sometimes ground meal, etc., coloured with a dye obtained from the bakam or sappan-wood tree. *Gulāl* is usually red, though sometimes of other colours. Nanddās here imagines Manasij 'the mind-born one', i.e. the god of love Kāmdev, as taking part in the spring festival of Holī, in which *gulāl* is thrown about in great quantities.

170 Kāmdev: See preceding note.

178 whose melody . . .: The melody of Krishna's flute is regarded as an expression of his *yogamāyā* or divine creative power, through which in his *aiśvarya* he evolves the universe. It is Krishna's flute which voices the mystery of *brahman*, which otherwise can only be enunciated in paradoxes such as that of the 'unstruck sound' or *anāhad nād*. Such paradoxes are often used, e.g. by the Hindi poet Kabīr, to stress the *nirguṇ* quality of the ultimate reality. Nanddās makes this quality depend in the last resort upon Krishna.

197 Love's essence: The herdgirls are *suddha premamaya rūpa* 'forms, or beings, of pure love'.

225 *Sāvan:* The name of a month which falls during the monsoon period.

29 had now to their proper places flown: They are restored by Krishna's supernatural power. The reference as it stands strengthens the notion of the perfection and the spiritual significance of Krishna's *līlā*. The *Purāṇa's* version is simpler, there being no mention there of restoration of the ornaments; Nanddās is no doubt trying to de-emphasise the suggestion of physical passion as between the Braj wives and Krishna. See p. 41, n. 2 for other examples of this.

231 Parīkṣit: The *Purāṇa* at this point merely makes Parīkṣit ask how the herdgirls escaped the cycle of birth and rebirth. Nanddās's Parīkṣit is not concerned with this abstract question, however. Much more a devotee of the *saguṇa* god or avatār, he is reluctant to think that devotion may not lead directly to Krishna.

Nanddās stresses again in Śuka's answer to Parīkṣit that the girls' love for Krishna is not earthly love, but love for the divine, of whose being they alone have full experience.

235 one whom Kānha kept . . . : Parīkṣit refers to himself here. His birth, devotion and benevolent rule are described in *Bhāgavata Purāṇa* I. 12.

239 Śyām: 'the dark one'; a name of Krishna.

251 Śiśupāl: An inveterate enemy of Krishna during his life and in previous incarnations, who ultimately recognised his divinity in his heart of hearts. As he died he thought of Krishna, and this was sufficient to win him salvation. Krishna abducted Śiśupāl's bride-to-be, Rukmiṇī. *Vishnu Purāṇa* IV. 15. 1–12, *Bhāgavata Purāṇa* X. 52–54, etc.

255 Hari's love: *Hari rasa*. See note to l. 59 above.

257 Govind: A name of Vishnu-Krishna.

258 lotus eyes: The central idea here is that the girls' love awakens at Krishna's as lotuses (certain species) unfold in the moonlight.

260 Hari's inner eye: Nanddās imagines the corners of Hari's *mana naina* 'inner eye' drawing out towards his ear, which alone so far tells him that the girls are approaching.

268 twin partridges: Krishna gazes at the girls' faces as a partridge (which is said to live only on moonbeams' nectar) gazes longingly at the moon. The girls' faces are as beautiful as the moon itself, it is implied.

278 passion: The *ujjvala rasa* 'glowing delight' of love for the divine, which Krishna here encourages. See p. 24, n. 27.

300 Giridhar: 'mountain-holder'; a name of Krishna, commemorating his lifting up of Govardhan Hill to shelter the people and herds of Braj from torrential rains sent by Indra, who was jealous of their worship of Krishna. *Bhāgavata Purāṇa* X. 24–5.

312 the Law: *dharma;* see note to l. 135.

315 calling on God's name: *japa*. The word *japa* denotes the practice of repeating constantly a word or formula as an aid to concentrating the attention on the ultimate being or reality. Very often it is the name of a deity that is repeated in this way, e.g. Hari, or Rām. *Japa* may take the form of mere outward observance, but is also considered to be an aspect of an inner concentration of the faculties upon the ultimate.

The importance of the divine name as a symbol of the ultimate being and the efficacy of invoking it are more stressed among devotees of Rām and those of a *nirguṇa*, unqualified supreme being (as worshipped by Kabīr and his sect) than in the *saguṇa*-oriented north Indian cult of Krishna. The name offered the possibility of a more abstract approach to the divine being than this form of Krishna worship usually required, but nonetheless it was important in north Indian Krishna worship. Sūrdās has several *padas* on the value of *sumirana* 'remembrance', the recollection (or *japa*) of the divine name or names; to him *sumirana* or *japa* conduce at least in part to a realisation of the nature of his *saguṇa* Krishna. Verses in point here are *Sūrsāgar*, ed. cit., I, no. 115, stressing the qualities and form of Krishna and his name as being Śyāma-Hari, and no. 82 in which the function of the avatārs of Vishnu-Krishna is stressed. The name of Hari is by far the most important to Sūr, that of Rām less so on the whole, though occasionally it is given the highest value (as when it is said, verse no. 231, to contain the essence of the divine being). See ed. cit., I, nos. 344–51; 57; 89–93; 231; 232–5; and further on the divine name, F. R. Allchin, 'The place of Tulsī Dās in north Indian devotional tradition', *Journal of the Royal Asiatic Society*, 1966, pp. 132 ff.; on the Name in Sikhism, W. H. McLeod, *Gurū Nānak and the Sikh Religion*, Oxford, 1968, pp. 150, etc.

Nanddās in the present line indicates the limited utility of *japa* in comparison with the incomparable form of Krishna himself. He later mentions *sumirana*, see translation, l. 800, and note.

332 in these three worlds: See note to *Bhramargīt*, l. 126.

337 Nandlāl: 'Nand's darling, or son', i.e. Krishna.

339 in himself content: *ātmarāma*. Krishna is presented here as essentially self-dependent or self-immanent, not looking beyond himself to the herdgirls, or to the world. The term *ātmārām* has an essentially *nirguṇ* reference, and is hence of marginal importance to Vaishnavas of *saguṇ* persuasion. See Ch. Vaudeville, *L'Invocation*, Paris, 1969, pp. 62 ff.

344 sandal: sandalwood, i.e. sandalwood oil or perfume.

353 Balbīr: A name of Krishna.

359 *vīnā:* The *vīṇā*, a large stringed instrument of the general type of the lute, in which gourds are mounted as resonators at either end of the finger-board.

361 *campā*: *Michelia*, a yellowish white, fragrant, conical-shaped flower, from which a perfume is made.

367 amaranths: Plants of this genus are well known for their

yellow, red and purple flowers. Several are cultivated or grow wild on the Indian plains and the Himalayan foothills.

367 *ketkīs*: The *kevṛā*, or *ketkī*, is the screwpine (*Pandanus odoratissimus*), a well-known plant with fragrant spikes of flowers, from which a perfume is made.

369 basils: The shrub basil (*Ocimum basilicum*) is revered by Vaishnavas. It is often planted in courtyards of houses, etc., and necklaces of beads of its wood are sometimes worn.

371 lilies: *kamoda*. Nanddās is probably referring to the white water-lily or lotus, *kumuda*, the seeds of which (*kamal-gaṭṭā*) are said in Ayurvedic medicine to act as a sexual invigorant or as an aphrodisiac, among other functions. The *Purāṇa* mentions *kumudas* at this juncture (X. 29.45), but only in connection with their fragrance, and the alteration is probably Nanddās's own.

The reference is conceivably to a different plant, the tree *Mallotus phillipinensis* (*Rottlera tinctoria*); this provides a drug known as *kamūd* (though more usually as *kamelā*, etc., or as *kamala* 'lotus') which shares several properties with *kumuda* seeds. Some confusion of the drugs in question is apparent in these names. The properties in question seem if anything to be more firmly associated with *kumuda* seeds, cf. *Āyurvedīy viśva-koṣ*, ed. R. J. Siṃha and D. J. Siṃha, Etawah, 1942, pp. 2159–73, 2179–85.

385 Madan: A name of Kāmdev; see note to l. 170.

388 Passion: *Rati*; the name of a wife of Kāmdev.

457 *kadamba*: A tree (*Nauclea cadamba*) common in the Braj region, and sacred to Krishna.

457 *neem*: The margosa (*Melia Azadirachta*), a tree whose seeds, bark and wood have many uses; it is well-known for its bitter-tasting sap and fruit.

467 the butter-thief: Krishna; a reference to one of his childhood pranks in stealing freshly-made butter or curd from the housewives of Braj, especially Yaśodā.

470 *tulsī*: basil; see note to l. 369.

481 act out his capture of their hearts: An illustration of their absorption in Krishna, heightened by the separation (*virah*) from him which he is causing them to endure.

487 . . . the grub lies numb . . .: This is an allusion to the ichneumon fly which stings and immobilises, then lays its eggs in the bodies of caterpillars or grubs, out of which its

larvae hatch. The caterpillar is supposed to be obsessed by fear at the pain of the sting, or to be 'meditating' on the fly, and so to transform itself into the fly. Cf. G. A. Grierson, *Padumāwati*, Calcutta, 1911, p. 49; Vaudeville, *Pastorales*, p. 145.

494 wheel, conch, lotus, mace: The usual emblems of Vishnu. Statues or idols of many of the forms of Vishnu carry one of these emblems in each of their four hands, and can be identified by their respective arrangement. A connection of the wheel or discus of Vishnu with the thunderbolt (*vajra*) is possible, cf. Gonda, *Aspects of Early Viṣṇuism*, p. 98; also following note.

495 thunderbolt: A weapon properly belonging to the Vedic god Indra. The Vedic Vishnu assisted Indra in his fight with the demon Vṛtra, and as the supreme being is sometimes represented as carrying Indra's thunderbolt, See further note to l. 124 above.

501 a rival's tracks: The herdgirls' unnamed rival would appear to represent Rādhā, to whom Nanddās gives no explicit place in his version of the story. See p. 43.

508 a crystal mirror . . .: Krishna and his consort cannot bear living out of each other's sight. This motif is found in Parīkh's edition of the *vārtā* of Kumbhandās (Barz, op. cit., p. 276), one of the members of the *aṣṭ chāp* associated with Vallabha, where a companion of Rādhā's is represented as holding the mirror while Krishna, seated on a raised dais, braids her hair as a preliminary to the *rās* dance. In including the motif here Nanddās is certainly influenced by the strength of the popular tradition of Rādhā, and perhaps by the Rādhā-Vallabha cult.

525 saints: The word *sant*, here rendered 'saints', means basically 'an essentially good or pious person'. It usually refers, as here, to persons of religious vocation, especially *sādhus* or 'holy men'. Sometimes in north India it refers specifically to devotees such as Kabīr, whose *bhakti* is to a supreme being regarded as unqualified and without avatārs. See further W. H. McLeod, *Gurū Nānak and the Sikh Religion*, pp. 151 ff.

536 gleaming gold: A reference to Rādhā's traditionally golden complexion is to be seen here.

554 a second best: The girls are conscious that Rādhā is the divine *śakti* of Krishna. See p. 43, n. 5

559 Indirā: See note to l. 79.

565 flood and flame: References to Krishna's lifting up Govardhan Hill (see note to l. 300), and to his swallowing up a forest fire that once threatened the people of Braj. *Bhāgavata Purāṇa* X. 17.

566 serpent's bane: The poison of Kāliya, a hundred-headed snake which lived in the river Jumna. Krishna fought, defeated and banished it. *Bhāgavata Purāṇa* X. 16.

570 Yaśodā: Krishna's fostermother, the wife of Nand. In the *Purāṇa* Krishna is the son of Vasudeva and Devakī, daughter of the tyrant king Kaṃsa of Mathura. Devakī's first several children are all killed in infancy by Kaṃsa because of his fear of a prophecy that a son of hers (Krishna) will slay him. When Krishna was born, Vasudeva, through the agency of *yogamāyā* (see note to l. 178), escaped through the locked doors of the confinement room and past the guards of the palace to Gokul in Braj, where he substituted him for a daughter of Yaśodā's born on the same night. This daughter was in reality a further manifestation of *yogamāyā*. Krishna's elder brother Balrām had earlier been transferred, while still unborn, from Devakī's womb to that of Rohiṇī, another wife of Vasudeva, in Braj. In this way the two half-brothers were brought to the village scene of their exploits, while at the same time the tradition of Krishna's princely origin among the Yādavas was maintained.

572 Brahmā: As distinct from the impersonal *brahman*, or *brahmă* (as the word appears in certain Sanskrit contexts, and usually in Hindi) there exists a deity Brahmā, who is regarded as a manifestation of *brahman* in personal form as the creator of the universe. The word *vidhi* 'ordinance, destiny' is used as a common title of Brahmā, as here by Nanddās. Brahmā, Vishnu, and Śiva were regarded from a fairly early date as forming a loose triad of deities who preside respectively over the creation, preservation and ultimate dissolution of the universe in each of its successive *kalpas* or phases of existence. Nanddās here makes the herdgirls ask Brahmā for the birth of Vishnu-Krishna to enact his function in this scheme.

599 yellow robe, and garland . . .: Krishna's robe is traditionally yellow or saffron-coloured, and one of his many titles,

Vanamālī, describes him as wearing a garland of forest flowers.

615 crisscross lightning: The girls' lighter-coloured hands or arms, laid against Krishna's dark robe and body. Fair complexion is regarded as a mark of beauty.

622 Lord Hari sat . . .: As many Krishnas now appear as there are herdgirls, so that each may enjoy complete communion with him.

638 love's ways: The idea behind these verses is that love (*bhakti*) offers the only true approach to Krishna, whether expressed conventionally through sectarian worship with the singing of his praises, etc., or otherwise. The question put by the herdgirls in the second verse here is a rhetorical one; the girls do not expect to be told any more of love than they already know.

656 my power . . .: Vishnu spreads out the universe by deploying the *guṇas* through his *yogamāyā*, or divine creative power; cf. *Bhāgavata Purāṇa* III. 19.17, and note to l. 178.

663 cows of plenty: The *kāmadhenu* is a cow supposed to be the source of satisfaction of all desires.

670 lotus: See note to l. 117.

672 the emerald glow . . .: The contrasting colours of Krishna's dark body, which is often described as bluish or greenish, and the light-complexioned bodies of the girls; there is doubtless a hidden reference to the golden body of Rādhā also.

686 cloud: The dark colour of monsoon clouds is symbolic of that of Krishna.

699 secret signs: By these are meant the involuntary hints given by Krishna of his emotions. These are the *sāttvika bhāvas* of rhetorical theory. They comprise sweating, weeping, horripilation and so forth.

707 transcendental light: The adjective used is *adbhuta* 'supernatural, marvellous'. Nanddās reverts to the idea that the herdgirls are not to be regarded as mere earthly women, and implies that their love should be seen as an idealisation of human love.

713 *pān*: Betel leaf, and the substances chewed with it such as areca nut, lime, etc. Here the red juice produced in the chewing of *pān* is meant.

717 the sacred texts: *nigama-āgama*, a loose expression designating

the original Vedic texts (see note to l. 792) and their derived literature.

723 *rāg* and *rāginī*: *rāgas* are certain musical modes or associations of notes, *rāgiṇīs* others thought of as their 'female' counterparts, with which they may blend to evoke a variety of moods.

728 its charm not of this world: The dance is *adbhuta rasa* 'of ineffable, or supernatural savour'.

763 Sanaka, Sanandan: Two of the four 'mind-born' sons of Brahmā, and companions of Vishnu.

763 Śārdā: A name of Sarasvatī, the goddess of speech and learning. She is sometimes described as daughter or wife of Brahmā.

764 Nārada: A *ṛṣi* or sage to whom some Vedic hymns are credited. He is sometimes described as a son of Brahmā; also as the inventor of the *vīṇā*, a Gandharva (see note to l. 104) and a friend of Krishna.

765 birthless god: *Aja*; a title applied to Brahmā and also to other gods.

768 lotus goddess: *Kamalā*; a name of Lakṣmī, who is associated in different ways with the lotus.

775 the soul: the *antaryāmī;* see p. 22.

781 true love, God's grace: *prema bhakti.* See p. 22.

786 Hari's love: *Hari dharma;* see note to l. 135. We see reflected in this remark something of the Vaishnava sense of identity within Hindu society. Both orthodox Hindus adhering to brahmanical rites and others could be Vaishnavas. From the *Bhaktmāl's* reference to Nanddās we may suspect that he was by inclination himself not strongly opposed to orthodoxy, though his statements in his *Bhramargīt* show that he fully recognised the potential liberating effect of *Hari dharma.*

792 Vedas: Both the earliest works produced by the Indo-Aryans in India (the 'Vedic texts' in the strictest sense) and the later commentaries and philosophical speculations deriving from them are included in the term *nigama*, used here.

799 tales . . . name: *śravaṇa*, listening to the legends of Krishna, *kīrtana*, praising Krishna in devotional songs, and *sumirana*, invoking Krishna's name or names; the first three aspects

of the 'ninefold *bhakti*' of the *Bhāgavata Purāṇa*, see p. 23, n. 25. On *sumirana*, see also note to l. 315 above.

801 Vedas: The reference here is to the Vedas as *śruti*, things 'heard' by divine revelation. Texts composed and passed down by men are in the orthodox brahmanical view *smṛti* 'remembered', and include the *Purāṇas*. Nanddās is saying here that Krishna's *rāslīlā* has a universal significance surpassing (though it of course includes) that of the Vedas.

802 they vanquish sin, and charm the heart . . .: A progression leading to the devotee's attainment of perfect love (*prem*).

Bhramargīt

6 love's delight: *rasa*. See note to *Rāspancādhyāyī* (*Rp.*), l. 59.

7 Śyām: See note to *Rp.*, l. 239.

11 no chance have I found: The phrase refers to the *Bhāgavata Purāṇa* context of the story, in which Uddhav first visits Krishna's fosterparents Nand and Yaśodā, only meeting the herdgirls the following day; see Introduction, p. 49.

16 Nandlāl: See note to *Rp.*, l. 337.

27 their honoured guest: The ceremonial welcome of a guest is referred to here. Various *upacāras* or forms of attention (sometimes sixteen) are prescribed, including the giving of water, and *pān* (see note to *Rp.*, l. 713), washing the feet, and circumambulation of the guest.

33 Balbīr: See note to *Rp.*, l. 353.

35 Balrām: See note to *Rp.*, l. 570.

36 Yadu kin: The Yādavas or descendants of Yadu; a clan or tribe inhabiting the district of Braj at an early period, with whom the names of Vāsudev and Krishna are connected. (See p. 12, n. 8).

38 on this bank: i.e. in Braj (across the river from Mathura).

43 Mohan: See note to *Rp.*, l. 129.

61 What light of Brahma? The reference here and elsewhere in these verses (except at ll. 92 and 112) is to the impersonal *brahman* or *brahma*; see note to *Rp.*, l. 572. The herdgirls do not follow Uddhav's form of words exactly in their rejoinder; it may be that Nanddās is implying that they do not give his views quite the attention they deserve, see p. 49, n. 4. On the other hand he is

perhaps merely setting the tone here for the girls' general impatience with Uddhav's views.

67 his flute: See note to *Rp.*, l. 178.

70 attributes . . . : Uddhav denies the herdgirls' assertion that Mohan's form is ultimately real; it is, he says, *saguṇa* or qualified, Mohan's eye, ear, voice etc. being aspects or attributes, *upādhi*, of its qualified nature. To Uddhav, Krishna is a *nirguṇ*, negatively defined, changeless principle, beyond the three *guṇas* (the qualities of *sattva* 'being, goodness', *rajas* 'passion' and *tamas* 'darkness' whose interaction produces the phenomenal world).

80 who ate the butter? A reference to Krishna as *mākhan-cor*, the butter-thief. See note to *Rp.*, l. 467.

83 collyrium: Lampblack, ointment or pigment smeared round the eyes or on the eyelashes as a cosmetic, or for medicinal reasons.

85 Govardhan hill: See note to *Rp.*, l. 300.

85 f. Yaśodā and Nand: See note to *Rp.*, l. 570.

87 Kānha: See note to *Rp.*, l. 33.

92 the egg of Brahmā: The 'cosmic egg' from which sprang the lotus that in turn gave birth to Brahmā, the creator of the universe. According to the *Bhāgavata Purāṇa* (XI. 24.9 f.) the Lord (*Bhagavān*) created this egg from cosmic matter and entered it to give birth to Brahmā.

93 He took man's shape . . . A reference to the avatār Krishna, a manifestation of the divine being on earth in human form. Ten avatārs or 'descents' of Vishnu are enumerated, of which the seventh and eighth, Rām and Krishna, are the most important; the tenth, called Kalkī, is still awaited. By performing their acts in the world the avatārs carry out the preservative functions of Vishnu (see note to *Rp.*, l. 572). In the case of Rām and Krishna these acts are often referred to as their *līlā* 'pleasure or will'.

95 yoga: The word *yoga* means 'union' or 'joining' and is cognate with the English word *yoke*. As used here, and usually, it denotes practices of meditation and concentration aimed at bringing the soul into a state of union with the divine being. The physical side of *yoga*, with its exercises and postures, is thought of as assisting this activity of mind and spirit.

96 highest Brahma's city . . .: The idea is that Śyām, whom the herdgirls think of in *saguṇa*, personal terms, is equatable

with and only to be found in the impersonal, supreme *brahman* (*brahma*).

101 Nandanandana: 'Nand's delight, or son'; a name of Krishna.

101 Nandanandana's reality: The word *guṇa* is rendered in this verse as 'reality' and in the following line as 'proof of his being'. The girls urge Uddhav to see Krishna as a *saguṇa* entity as they themselves do, and insist in the second part of the verse that merely to contemplate Mohan will convince a right-thinking person of his *saguṇa* nature.

A slightly different sense may be read into the verse by taking the word *guṇa* in its common derived sense 'virtues'. The general drift of the girls' argument remains the same.

108 Śiva: The reference here is to the god Śiva as the greatest of ascetics, the perfection of whose asceticism reflects his divine power. Śiva is often thought of as the supreme god, and with his consciousness of the value of *yoga* Uddhav may all the more readily see Hari as an aspect of Śiva at this point in the argument.

110 *karma*: The word *karma* means 'action'. It is used here, as often, in the sense of action as viewed in the light of the dictates of religion and society; acts which are good in these terms increase merit and so shorten the succession of births and rebirths through which the soul must pass before attaining *mukti* 'release'. Of wrongful acts the reverse is true. This is the so-called 'law of *karma*', which Uddhav upholds and which the girls strenuously deny.

113 fourteen worlds . . . The earth and six heavenly regions above it, with seven below. Sometimes the seven upper worlds only are mentioned, sometimes only three worlds (see following note). The highest heaven is that of Brahmā, from which souls are not born again. The 'seven isles' are the *sapta dvīpa* or seven divisions of the world, i.e. the whole world. The expression *nava khaṇḍa* 'nine continents' has the same sense.

126 three worlds: *tribhuvana*, heaven, earth, and the intermediary regions (or on a different reckoning, the lower world).

131 Repose in Brahma's realm: Release, and the repose which release brings, proceed from consciousness of the identity of the self (*ātmā*) with the impersonal *brahman* (*brahma*). A prerequisite of such consciousness is the acquisition of good *karma* from earlier births.

144 the lotus pose: *padmāsana*, a yogic posture. The aim of meditation is visualised as the stilling of the senses and drawing up of the vital energies progressively from the loins towards the brain, with the nine orifices of the body closed; complete success is said to allow the escape of the spirit through a 'tenth door' which opens inside the skull, whereupon the spirit merges with the absolute.

152 Śyāmsundar: 'Śyām the beautiful'; a name of Krishna.

159 Vedas: See notes to *Rp.*, ll. 792 and 801. The Vedas' 'negative' is the Upanishadic phrase *neti neti* 'not this, not this', expressing the impossibility of defining the supreme spirit in positive terms.

160 Upanishads: See Introduction, pp. 9 f.

161 The Self: The *ātmā*; see note to l. 131 above.

167 qualities: The herdgirls reassert their conviction that the ultimate being must be positively qualified, and the Vallabhan view that Krishna deploys the universe by obscuring aspects of his divine nature (see Introduction, p. 21); they use the term *māyā*, translated 'illusion' here, and 'error' in the following verse, to describe men's lack of comprehension of this process. The phenomena of the world may not in fact be exactly as they seem, but are nevertheless real, partaking of the infinite positive qualities of Krishna.

Uddhav's answer is that if the supreme being (whom he agrees to call Hari) is indeed said to possess qualities, these are undefinable; the supreme being thus has certain similarities for him to the unqualified being of the Upanishads and Śaṅkara's view (see Introduction, pp. 9f., 15f.). For Uddhav the apparent qualities of the phenomenal world which *māyā* reveals are not aspects or qualities of this being. This viewpoint is reconcilable with the philosophy of Vallabha, which admits the notion of a *nirguṇa* being whose qualities differ from those of the world (see p. 21). Uddhav seems here to be urging a refinement of the Vallabhan view overlooked by the girls—one, perhaps, not uncongenial to Nanddās, see p. 49, n. 4.

184 The Vedas? The Vedas are comprehended in Hari, say the girls. See note to *Rp.*, l. 801.

192 Love is a craving . . .: Uddhav says here that love (*prem*) for the divine being, whom he calls *Bhagavān* (see note to *Rp.*, l. 135), hardly comes into question if the latter is

'beyond all qualities' and less comprehensible than even the distant sun or moon (which do possess qualities).

209 devotion: The word used is *bhakti*.

217 *Karm*'s a vain bond . . .: *Karma* can have no meaning, say the girls, if (as is the case) Hari is not subject to it. That which is *nirguṇa* can only be subordinate to the *saguṇa* Hari, and could no doubt be regarded as a sort of *pramāṇa* or means of obtaining knowledge of him, were it not that Hari as the supreme being may not be known completely through rational enquiry. Could creation be *saguṇa* in any case, they ask triumphantly, if the ultimate being were *nirguṇa*? The herdgirls are unshakeable in their convictions, and give Uddhav's point of view less credence in this curious verse than he has done theirs in the verse preceding.

227 Vāsudev: The Bhāgavata god identified with Vishnu-Krishna. See Introduction, p. 10.

232 the babe reborn: The reference is to Krishna as Adhokṣaj 'born under the axle'; this title is explained by the *Harivaṃśa* to mean that the baby Krishna's destruction of the demoness Pūtanā (see n. to l. 296) was so miraculous that he was considered to have been 'born again', under the axle of the cart on which she had settled to poison him.

240 a tiny plum: *āmalaka*, the small plum-like fruit of Emblic myrobalan (*Phyllanthus emblica*). It is used in dyeing and tanning.

244 vision of Nandlāl: In this vision, and again towards the end of the poem, Nanddās expresses the mystical ecstasy to which *bhakti* is said to be able to lead. Within Hindi literature this strain of *bhakti* is, however, more typical on the whole of such a figure as the poetess Mīrābāī (see Introduction, p. 20) than of Nanddās.

260 Krishna's flute: See note to *Rp.*, l. 178.

261 Why linger far off . . .: The verse refers to Krishna's absence in Mathura, beyond the woods of Vṛndāvan; its imagery and that of the next verse recall Krishna's disappearance in the forest during his *rāslīlā*.

282 You've struck down . . .: The girls complain here of Krishna's supposed harshness in abandoning them, and in later verses describe similar instances of his harshness and indifference towards his devotees in earlier incarnations. This is the motif of their *upālambh* 'reproach', which is

prominent in treatments of the *bhramargīt* theme from the *Purāṇa* onwards, see Introduction, pp. 52f.

287 fiery bane . . . : For the references in this verse see notes to *Rp.*, ll. 565, 566.

290 young laughing Nand: The name Nand 'joy' is applied to Krishna as well as to Nand, his fosterfather.

293 sin and merit: The qualities of *pāp* and *puṇya* as deriving from actions (*karm*).

296 Pūtanā: An infanticide and abortion-causing demoness who in the *Bhāgavata Purāṇa* took the form of a woman intending to kill the infant Krishna with her poisoned milk. (*Bhāgavata Purāṇa* X. 6.)

300 *Rāmcandra*: The avatār Rām, fabled to be descended from an ancestor Raghu of the solar race (as Krishna and the Yādavas are of the lunar race). The demoness Tāṛakā was killed by Rām as he was journeying to the hermitage of the sage Viśvāmitra, whose sacrifice had been interfered with by demons. The Sanskrit *Rāmāyaṇa* which provides the basis for the story stresses Ram's reluctance to kill a female (I. 25); Nanddās's treatment is more reminiscent of that of Tulsīdās in his *Rāmcaritmānas* (I. 209), and of the Sanskrit *Adhyātma Rāmāyaṇa*, a work on which Tulsīdās drew to a large extent, probably dating from the fifteenth century A.D.

308 the high Law: 'the supreme (*parama*) *dharma*'; see note to *Rp.*, l. 135. In his avatār as Rām or Rāmcandra, prince of Ayodhyā, the god dutifully endured a long banishment from the kingdom which was brought about by intrigue (divinely engineered) on the part of a maidservant and one of the king's wives. Despite this trait he showed great harshness to women, says Nanddās. Śūrpanakhā was a demoness who fell in love with Rām while he, his wife Sītā, and Laksmaṇ his brother were living in exile in the forest. When Rām rejected her advances she attacked Sītā, and her ears and nose were cut off by Lakṣmaṇ at Rām's instigation, says the Sanskrit *Rāmāyaṇa* which provides the basis of the story. The *Bhāgavata Purāṇa* in one reference makes Rām himself Sītā's avenger (IX. 10.9). In instancing Śūrpanakhā's treatment here Nanddās seems to be following the *Purāṇa*, but perhaps with some hesitation, as the latter part of the verse does not mention Rām by name.

318 flowerdecked: *vanamālī* 'wearing a garland of forest flowers'; an epithet of Vishnu-Krishna, and associated with his Vāman avatār (see following note).

319 Bali the king: A king of the race of Daityas, demons and giants, who by his sacrifices obtained dominion over the three worlds with the status of Indra. At the gods' request Vishnu appeared before him, assuming his Vāman or dwarf avatār. When Bali granted the dwarf as much land as he could step over in three paces the latter grew to gigantic size and stepped across earth and heaven in two paces; the lower world he left to Bali. *Bhāgavata Purāṇa* VIII. 15, 18–21.

325 Prahlād: Bali's father. His own father, Hiraṇyakaśipu, had through his austerities been granted a boon by Brahmā that he should not be killed by any created being, after which he conquered all the worlds and ruled from Indra's palace in heaven. Prahlād's stubborn devotion to Vishnu as a child infuriated his father, who tried to have him killed by various means, but unsuccessfully. When Hiraṇyakaśipu denied the existence of an omnipresent lord of the universe, Vishnu burst out of a pillar in his palace in the form of Nṛsiṃha, a creature part man and part lion, and killed him. *Bhāgavata Purāṇa* VII. 3–8.

333 Paraśurām: 'Rām the axe-bearer'; the sixth avatār of Vishnu, following Nṛsiṃha and Vāman. Paraśurām is depicted as a brahman, the son of a sage called Jamadagni. He killed his mother Reṇukā at the instance of Jamadagni, who suspected her virtue. His hostility to the *kṣatriyas* or 'warriors', who comprise with the brahmans the two upper *varṇas* or broad divisions of early Indo-Aryan society, is said to reflect early struggles for power between these groups. When Jamadagni was killed by *kṣatriyas* in the course of a feud Paraśurām resolved to exterminate all *kṣatriyas*, and according to the *Bhāgavata Purāṇa* (IX. 15.14; 16.19) carried out this task 21 times over. The name Samantapancaka contains a reference to the five lakes or pools filled with their blood which he is supposed to have made, and stood in to perform a sacrifice (*Mahābhārata* I. 2.4–11).

342 Śiśupāl: A king of the Cedi tribe, selected by King Bhīṣmak of Vidarbha as the future husband for his daughter, Rukmiṇī; she, however, loved Krishna, and Krishna

wished to marry her. On hearing that her marriage to Śiśupāl was to take place she sent a message to Krishna, who came with Balrām and abducted her despite great opposition, and with some of the Yādavas defeated the army sent in pursuit. *Bhāgavata Purāṇa* X. 52–4.

357 knowledge pure: Nanddās refers here to the idea that attainment to the perfection of love brings complete attainment to Krishna, with all that this signifies. See Introduction, p. 22, and note to l. 564 below.

407 pilfered curd: The girls see Uddhav, the bee, as a thief stealing his doctrines wherever he can find them in the world beyond Braj, just as a bee steals honey from the flowers. There is also an echo of Krishna in the symbolism here, however. The dark Krishna too was a thief of curds in his childhood in Braj, and the girls are sure that Krishna the youth is now flitting from one love to another in Mathura.

414 black body, yellow face: Black and yellow are said to be associated traditionally with the *śūdra* and *vaiśya varṇas* of early Indo-Aryan society, i.e. those ritually inferior to the *brāhmaṇ* and *kṣatriya varṇas.*

448 horned like brute beasts: The girls imagine the bees' antennae as horns of cattle or buffaloes.

459 reaching the true Self: *ātama siddhi* 'self-realisation'.

462 existential argument: *niguna niranai* 'inference about the unqualified'.

466 Shyām's unconditioned power: *nirguna sakti*; see Introduction, p. 21. The word 'condition' in the following line answers to *saguna* of the original.

470 the hunchback: Trivakrā 'thrice deformed'; a beautiful maidservant of Kaṃsa, whom Krishna and Balrām met when they came to Mathura from Braj for the purpose of killing Kaṃsa. Krishna was pleased by her and removed her deformity. She begged him to visit her at her house and he jokingly agreed to do so. To Sūrdās's and Nanddās's herdgirls the hunchback is a prime object of their jealousy. *Bhāgavata Purāṇa* X. 42.

498 Murāri: 'the enemy of Mura (a Daitya)', i.e. Krishna. Another name of Krishna, *Tribhaṅgī* 'broken in three', refers to the angular positions of his body and legs as he stands to play his flute, and allows the herdgirls a further sardonic reference to Krishna and the hunchback.

504 Govinda's Lay: The *Gītagovinda*, see Introduction, p. 18.

509 Keśav: A name of Krishna, referring to his hair (*keśa*).

512 a flood of tears: The idea of the ocean of tears drowning the weeping girls' eyes is suggestive, in English literature, of the style of such a poet as Crashaw, who was also trying to express the soul's mystical longing for union with the divine. Cf. Crashaw's poem *Saint Mary Magdalene;* also John Donne's *A Valediction: of Weeping.* Some similar conceits are found in the final verse of the present poem.

535 conventional ways: *marajāda*, *maryādā* 'propriety, morality'. For Vallabha and his sect *maryādā bhaktas* are the devotees who seek salvation by their own efforts, i.e. by following the path of orthodoxy. In this they are meritorious, but while remaining attached to *maryādā* cannot attain to God's full grace, *puṣṭi*, since their souls do not as yet share the *ānand*, or bliss, of his divine nature.

556 communion with the good: *sādhu saṅgati*; its great virtues are stressed by the *Purāṇa*, XI. 12.1 ff.

564 And he touched their feet . . .: Uddhav now sees the herdgirls as supremely blessed, and in his devotion to them he feels the same ecstasy as they in their love for Krishna, as well as their sense of indignation at the way Krishna has treated them. When he returns to Mathura and reproaches Krishna for his neglect, ecstatic love for the girls reawakens in Krishna's heart, and he is again conscious of the perfect identity of their beings with his own. Uddhav's final vision of Krishna as a herdgirl stresses this identity, which is the fundamental reason for the importance of the girls in Nanddās's view of *bhakti*.

618 instinct with a herdgirl's being . . .: See notes to ll. 512, 564.

635 Nanddās: Some *Bhramargīt* manuscripts read *jana mukunda* in this line, rather than *nandadāsa*. This reading seems to depend on a reference in the *Bhāgavata Purāṇa's* account (X. 47.61 f.) to the herdgirls as abandoning their kinsfolk (*-jana*), and worshipping or tending the lotus feet of Mukunda, i.e. Krishna, in Vṛndāvan. The word *jana* 'person' can carry the meaning 'servant'; reading *jana mukunda*, the sense of the line would be either 'the servant (i.e. Nanddās) is purified in Mukunda', or 'the servant (of Krishna), Mukunda, is purified'.

If the reading is accepted and the phrase taken in the first sense, it implies that Nanddās, or a scribe, has used a variation to his signature in this final verse of the poem, being conscious of the *Bhāgavata Purāṇa* context (and of the fact that the name or title Nanddās itself means 'servant of Krishna'). If the phrase is taken in the second sense, the probable implication is that Nanddās himself went under the name Mukund, or was considered by a scribe to have done so. It is interesting to note here that the colophon of one *Bhramargīt* manuscript, at least, attributes the poem to 'the poet Mukund', rather than to Nanddās. Scribal and editorial confusion here is not ruled out, see Gupta, *Aṣṭchāp aur vallabh sampradāy*, pp. 346 ff.; but there is again the fact that in a list of the *aṣṭ chāp* poets given in one of the minor vārtās, the *Śrī Govardhannāth jī ke prākaṭya kī vārtā*, our poet is said to be designated not Nanddās, but 'Vishnudās', see Śukla, *Nanddās*, I, pp. 17 f. This no doubt encourages the supposition that a name of Vaishnava colouring (such as Mukund) will have underlain our poet's usual designation Nanddās.

The above evidence does not allow a definite interpretation of the reading, or a conclusion as to whether it goes back to Nanddās's original text. It seems at present quite possible that it may do so.

638 Rich in love's sweet content: *premarasa punjinī* 'wealthy in love's savour'; see Introduction, pp. 44 f.

APPENDIX

The following tables give the line references in Śukla's edition (see p. 31, n. 4) for the *Rāspancādhyāyī* and *Bhramargīt* verses as translated. The figures in right hand columns refer to the edition, those in left hand columns to the translations.

Rāspancādhyāyī

1–41	1–22	461–465	293–294
42–46	25–26	466–487	297–306
47–53	29–32	488–503	313–320
54–61	37–40	504–554	323–350
62–116	43–70	555–561	355–358
117–139	75–86	562–585	361–372
140–188	91–114	586–616	385–406
189–222	119–134	617–659	417–442
223–226	137–138	660–661	445–446
227–230	141–142	661–671	449–454
231–265	147–164	672–726	463–495
266–281	167–174	727–752	531–544
282–322	181–200	753–756	547–548
323–327	203–204	757–764	575–578
328–332	201–202	765–767	581–582
333–344	217–222	768–771	579–580
345–371	227–240	772–794	583–594
372–456	243–286	795–805	597–602
457–460	289–290		

Bhramargīt

1–9	1–5	89–97	51–55
10–17	6–10	98–106	56–60
18–26	11–15	107–115	61–65
27–34	16–20	116–123	66–70
35–42	21–25	124–132	71–75
43–51	26–30	133–140	76–80
52–60	31–35	141–149	81–85
61–69	36–40	150–158	86–90
70–78	41–45	159–166	91–95
79–88	46–50	167–175	96–100

176–183	101–105	411–419	241–245
184–191	106–110	420–427	246–250
192–199	111–115	428–435	251–255
200–208	116–120	436–443	256–260
209–216	121–125	444–452	261–265
217–225	126–130	453–460	266–270
226–233	131–135	461–468	271–275
234–242	136–140	469–476	276–280
243–250	141–145	477–485	281–285
251–259	146–150	486–492	286–290
260–267	151–155	493–501	291–295
268–274	156–160	502–510	296–300
275–283	161–165	511–518	301–305
284–291	166–170	519–527	306–310
292–298	171–175	528–536	311–315
299–307	176–180	537–545	316–320
308–316	181–185	546–554	321–325
317–324	186–190	555–563	326–330
325–332	191–195	564–572	331–335
333–340	196–200	573–580	336–340
341–349	201–205	581–589	341–345
350–359	206–210	590–597	346–350
360–367	211–215	598–605	351–355
368–376	216–220	606–613	356–360
377–385	221–225	614–621	361–365
386–394	226–230	622–629	366–370
395–402	231–235	630–638	371–375
403–410	236–240		

INDEX